THE EASY PEASY GUIDE TO MONEY SKILLS FOR TEENS

The Easy Peasy Guide to Money Skills for Teens

7 Simple Habits to Effective Saving, Spending, Budgeting, Investing, and Developing Financial Literacy

Noah Hawkins

Published by Matthew Duke Associates 2025

Email: info@matthewdukeassociates.com
Website: www.matthewdukeassociates.com

Email: info@noahhawkins.com

ISBN (eBook): 978-1-917164-90-0

ISBN (Paperback): 978-1-917164-88-7

Paperback First Edition: 2025

Endorsement From a Certified Financial Planner CFP®

"This book is a must-read for every teen before they manage money, open their first bank account, or apply for a credit card. Noah Hawkins makes financial literacy simple to understand and easy to apply—by showing you powerful yet easy to adopt money habits.

As a CFP®, this book should be essential reading in every school. I've read countless teen finance books and as a busy mom, this is the only book I trust to teach my kids about real-world money skills."

–Tracey L Weston, CFP®
Certified Financial Planner

Editorial Reviews

"Finally — a money book that actually makes sense and isn't boring! The way it explains stuff is super clear and actually fun to read. The real-life examples and interactive challenges made it way easier to get, and I didn't feel dumb or lost like I usually do with finance books like this."
— Rebecca Clayton, 16-year-old reader

"I've always worried how little schools teach our kids about money. This book gave my daughter not just knowledge, but confidence—without overwhelming her. It's clear, simple, and actionable. What surprised me most was how much I learned too. The Discussion & Group Activity for Parents in each chapter enabled Rebecca & I to have serious and meaningful conversations about Money."
— Kimberly Clayton, Mother of Rebecca

"This book nailed it. It did wonders for our whole family. It gave Rebecca the tools and confidence to talk money, helped Kimberly feel comfortable discussing topics she once avoided, and even impressed me with how it simplified complex ideas without dumbing them down. It's a clear, practical guide that teaches and builds strong money habits."
— Glenn Clayton, Father of Rebecca

"This book gets it right. It doesn't just teach money; it teaches money mindset. As an Entrepreneur who built numerous businesses from the ground up, I only wish I'd had a book like this when I was a Teen."
— Trevor Owens, Entrepreneur

To my Beautiful Wife — Meredith
Thank you for being my rock.

Table of Contents

Introduction:

Why Money Skills Matter for Teens

Parents, teachers, mentors, and homeschoolers—do you ever feel like schools aren't teaching kids the financial skills they actually need?

You're not alone. According to a recent study, 93% of teens recognize the importance of financial literacy, yet a staggering 74% of them admit they don't feel prepared for it (Greenlight & Researchscape, 2022). The good news? Your teen's about to beat those odds.

With this book, they won't just "know" about money. They'll understand how to use it, grow it, and manage it—without needing a degree in economics or a spreadsheet obsession. And they'll do it all without falling asleep from boredom or zoning out from "financial jargon overload."

Meet Noah (That's Me)

Hello! I'm Noah, and before we dive right in, I want to briefly tell you a bit about why I wrote this book. See, when I was a teenager growing up in a middle-class home on the South Side of Chicago, money felt like some big mystery no one would ever take the time to explain. My parents worked hard, but we just didn't really talk about money—except when we didn't have enough of it.

No one ever explained to me how to manage money—how to budget, how to save, or how debt can sometimes quietly sneak up on you like a ninja. And school? It taught me algebra and Shakespeare, sure, but not how to open a bank account or avoid late fees!

I remember getting my first paycheck from a summer job. I felt like a millionaire for about five minutes. But then? Yes—I blew most of it on sneakers I didn't need, takeout food, and a phone upgrade I couldn't afford. The rest vanished into thin air, and I had nothing to show for it but buyer's remorse and a bank account on life support.

And then came college. Suddenly, I was introduced to this shiny new concept called *debt.* It was sold to me as freedom. Turns out, it was more like a trap with interest. I took out loans I didn't fully understand. I used credit cards like magic wands. And I made every money mistake in the book before I even knew the book *existed.*

It was frustrating. Embarrassing. And isolating.

But I started learning. I read. I asked questions. I made a thousand mistakes. And slowly, I figured out how money actually worked. I started building habits, not just knowledge. And I noticed something else: *most teens were in the exact same boat I'd been in.* These were bright, ambitious young teens, but they were held back—not by a lack of potential, but by a lack of real-world money skills.

That's why I wrote this book.

I've spent the last decade mentoring teens and young adults—through workshops, school programs, and community initiatives—helping them build real-world confidence and practical financial skills. And I've seen firsthand what happens when teens finally "get it": they start making smarter decisions, setting bigger goals, and believing they have control over their future.

Now, it's your turn.

Why This Book Is Different

Let me be clear: This isn't just another book telling you to "spend less" and "save more." You already know that. In fact, you've probably heard it a hundred times.

This book is about *doing.*

Inside, you'll find

- real-life scenarios that make the money lessons stick.
- reflective questions and action-based challenges at the end of each chapter to help you take immediate action.
- a flexible, self-paced approach—because not every teen learns in the same way.
- zero boring lectures (and zero complicated finance lingo!).

This isn't just a book you'll read—it's a book you'll experience. Think of it like learning to ride a bike. You wouldn't read 10 books about cycling and expect to become an expert —you'd hop on, wobble a bit, and maybe even fall. But eventually, before you know it, you'd find yourself cruising. That's the style we're going for here: learn by doing, not just reading.

So, each chapter is going to focus on one powerful habit. From money mindset to budgeting, saving, earning, investing, and even building your own financial independence roadmap, you'll not only know *what* to do, you'll actually *do it*—with confidence.

Even if you walk away with just a few new habits, trust me: you'll still be ahead of 95% of your peers when it comes to managing money. But I suspect you'll do more than that.

What You'll Walk Away With

By the end of this book, you'll know how to

- build smart money habits that stick for life.
- budget without the stress.

- save money while still enjoying your life.
- make smart decisions about spending, credit, and debt.
- understand investing in a way that actually makes sense.
- use money as a tool—not something that controls you.

And just for picking up this guide, you also get access to **five free exclusive bonuses**, as follows:

1. **Habit 8 and Habit 9:** These are two full bonus chapters inside this book:
    - *Habit 8 (Bonus): Financial Independence* – Learn how to build freedom now, not decades from now.
    - *Habit 9 (Bonus): Building Wealth With Technology* – Crypto, AI, digital wallets, and the tech that will shape your financial world.
2. **Printable Teen Budgeting Sheets & Goal Trackers:** Stay on top of your progress with tools you can use offline.
3. **Spreadsheet Budgeting Template:** For those who prefer to track their money digitally.
4. **The Easy Peasy AI Wealth Guide for Teens:** Discover how real teens are using artificial intelligence to earn, invest, and build wealth.
5. **The Educator & Parent's Discussion Toolkit:** A valuable resource for classrooms, youth groups, homeschoolers, and family discussions.

All these bonuses are completely free and automatically included with your copy of the book. To access them, simply scan the QR code in the free Bonuses download page.

A Final Word Before We Get Started

To every teen reading this: Thank you for choosing this book. I know you could be anywhere right now—scrolling, gaming, binge-watching—but you chose to invest in yourself. That's powerful. And honestly? That's *rare.*

And to the parents, teachers, mentors, and homeschoolers—thank you for being the kind of adult who believes teens are capable of real financial wisdom. You're the reason books like this get into the right hands.

My goal with *The Easy Peasy Guide to Money Skills for Teens* is simple: to give you a rock-solid foundation in money habits that actually make a difference. Not someday—but right now. I want you to have the skills I wish I had had at your age, so that you can skip the struggles and jump straight to success.

Because the truth is, you don't have to wait until you're an adult to take control of your money. You can start today. And you should, in fact! You must!

Picture this: You're 30 years old, living in a luxury penthouse with skyline views, or maybe a villa with a private pool, taking spontaneous trips to tropical islands. You're driving your dream car, financially free, and living life on your own terms.

You've already retired your parents early—giving back to the people who raised you—and now, you get to spoil your partner with the best life has to offer, every chance you get.

Meanwhile, your friends? Still broke. Drowning in debt. Asking around for loans—or worse, asking you for cash—promising they'll "*pay you back soon*" (but you know they won't). Why? because they made the same mistakes everyone else does.

The difference? You started early. You built the money habits that put you ahead, while they wasted time.

So, don't wait until it's too late. Flip the page now and start building the habits that will make you unstoppable.

You've got this.

–Noah Hawkins

How to Use This Book

For Teens, Parents, Educators, Mentors, and Homeschoolers

This isn't just a book to read—it's a book to *use*. Each chapter is designed to help teens build real money habits with clarity, confidence, and action. Whether you're reading this for yourself or guiding someone else, follow the steps below to make the most of your journey.

As you read through each chapter, I highly recommend you highlight any quotes, examples, tips or challenges that speak to you or hit home. These will become your personal go-to moments to revisit later, helping you refresh your learning and reinforce each habit over time.

If You're a Teen

Step 1: Start with one habit chapter at a time. There's no rush—just focus on fully understanding the core concept.

Step 2: At the end of the chapter, read the **Chapter Takeaway** to reinforce the main habit and understand the **Cue → Routine → Reward** (CRR) formula.

Step 3: Complete the **Interactive Challenge Section** in your own notebook. These include self-assessments, real-life scenarios, habit builders, and an action challenge.

Step 4: When you reach the chapters on saving, spending, or budgeting, start using:

- Bonus #2: Printable Budget Sheets
- Bonus #3: Spreadsheet Budget Planner

These tools help you apply what you've learned in a practical way.

Step 5: Don't skip **Bonus Habit 8** (Financial Independence) and **Bonus Habit 9** (Future Trends)—they're included in the book to help future-proof your money mindset.

Optional Guidance: *Stick with each habit chapter until you can honestly rate yourself a solid 4 out of 5 on the self-assessment before moving forward. For most teens, this takes around* ***1–3 weeks per chapter****—but go at your own pace.* ***Mastery matters more than speed.***

If You're a Parent

Step 1: Skim the **Theory** sections or **Chapter Takeaways** to stay up to speed with what your teen is learning.

Step 2: Use the **Interactive Challenge Section** to spark discussions—ask your teen what stood out or what they found tricky.

Step 3: Help them use **Bonus #2** and **Bonus #3** for budgeting and goal setting—these are practical tools for real-world learning.

Step 4: Use **Bonus #5: The Educator & Parent's Toolkit** to guide conversations, games, and roleplays. You can introduce these casually or use them for weekly check-ins.

Step 5: Celebrate small wins. Encouragement makes a big difference when building long-term habits.

Optional Guidance: *Encourage your teen to stick with each habit chapter until they can confidently rate themselves at least a* ***4 out of 5*** *on the self-assessment. For most teens, this takes around* ***1–3 weeks****, but progress varies—support them at their own pace.*

If You're an Educator or Homeschooler

Step 1: Treat each habit chapter as a complete lesson. Use the **Theory** section to teach, and the **Chapter Takeaway** to summarize key ideas.

Step 2: Assign the **Interactive Challenge Section** for solo or group work—it's ideal for PSHE (UK life skills) classes, SEL (U.S. emotional development) classes, life skills, or economics classes.

Step 3: Use **Bonus #5: The Educator & Parent's Toolkit** to run class discussions, group roleplays, and reflective exercises.

Step 4: Integrate **Bonus #2** (Printable Tools) into lessons about budgeting, saving, or setting goals.

Step 5: Encourage group-based habit challenges to boost peer learning and accountability.

Optional Guidance: *Recommend students to stick with each habit chapter until they can genuinely rate themselves* ***4 out of 5*** *or higher on the self-assessment. On average, each chapter may take* ***1–3 weeks*** *to fully absorb but allow flexibility for different learners.*

If You're a Mentor or Youth Worker

Step 1: Choose habit chapters based on your mentee's current needs—start where they're struggling or curious.

Step 2: Use the **Chapter Takeaway** and **Interactive Challenge Section** to prompt real conversations and set personal goals.

Step 3: Lean on **Bonus #5** for quick games, discussion questions, and relatable roleplays—these are great for 1:1 or group mentoring.

Step 4: Walk through **Bonus #2** or **Bonus #3** together to help your mentee budget, plan, and track progress.

Step 5: Celebrate milestones—no matter how small. Recognizing progress keeps teens motivated.

Optional Guidance: *Encourage your mentee to stick with each chapter until they can honestly score themselves a* ***4 out of 5*** *or higher on the self-assessment. Most teens reach this point in* ***1–3 weeks*** *but give them the freedom to move faster or slower based on their individual pace and needs.*

Download Your Free Bonuses Here

As a thank you for choosing *The Easy Peasy Guide to Money Skills for Teens*, I've included a set of free, exclusive bonuses below. These are here to help you put the lessons in this book into action and start building some real-world financial habits!

Bonus #1

Habit 8 & Habit 9 *(Included inside this book)*

This first bonus is made up of two additional habit chapters you'll find immediately after Habit 7. In short, they help you go beyond the core habits to explore financial independence and future trends like crypto, digital money, and AI. I like to think of them as your roadmap to long-term success and future-proofing your money mindset.

Bonus #2

Printable Teen Budget Sheets & Goal Trackers

A simple template to help you plan, track, and stay on top of your finances—offline and distraction-free.

Bonus #3

Spreadsheet Budgeting Template

A flexible digital tool for teens who prefer budgeting on a computer or mobile device.

Bonus #4

The Easy Peasy AI Wealth Guide for Teens

Discover how real teens are using artificial intelligence to earn, invest, and prepare for the future of money.

Bonus #5

The Educator & Parent's Discussion Toolkit

A structured resource for parents, teachers, homeschoolers, or mentors to guide discussions, lessons, and group learning based on the content in this book.

To access your bonuses, visit:

www.matthewdukeassociates.com/money-skills-for-teens

(or simply scan the QR code below)

Habit 1:

Building Your Money Mindset

Your mind is your most powerful tool. Want to know why some people are great with money and others struggle? It all starts in their heads.

Why Your Mindset Matters

Your mind is your most powerful tool. Believe me. In fact, want to know why some people seem naturally great with money while others always feel behind? It's not because one group is smarter or better at math. It's because of what's going on in their *heads*. That's right—it all starts with mindset.

Let's break that down.

Scarcity vs. Abundance: The Belief Battle That Shapes Your Wallet

Here's something most people don't realize: the way you *think* about money influences what you *do* with it. Let me explain.

When I was younger, I had what's called a **scarcity mindset**. It's kind of like this quiet voice in the back of your mind that says:

"There's never going to be enough."

"I can't afford that."

"People like me just don't get rich."

Sound familiar? It's not just about being broke—it's about feeling stuck. People with a scarcity mindset tend to avoid learning about money, procrastinate on financial goals, and get stuck in a cycle of "survive now, stress later."

But then there's the **abundance mindset**—and no, it's not about pretending you're a billionaire when your bank account says otherwise. It's about believing that **you can grow**, **you can learn**, and **you can improve** your financial future—even if things aren't perfect right now.

Let's do a quick comparison:

Scarcity Thinking	**Abundance Thinking**
"I'll never have enough."	"I'm learning how to manage what I have."
"I can't afford it."	"How can I afford it?"
"I'm just bad with money."	"I can learn to get better with money."

The phrase **"How can I afford it?"** is a game changer. See, instead of shutting down your brain with "I can't," it opens a door, it invites your mind to solve a problem. And that shift? It's the first step to building wealth.

Also, if you want a simple trick to start flexing that mindset muscle today? Try the **24-hour pause rule**.

Whenever you feel the urge to buy something online—like that viral hoodie or those noise-cancelling headphones that seem urgent but probably aren't—take a pause. Wait one full day before you click "buy now."

Why? Because most of the time, you'll realize you don't even want it anymore.

That one small habit flips you from chasing instant gratification to building intentional choices. And every time you wait instead of spending without thinking, you're strengthening your abundance mindset.

One of my students, Branden, used to think saving money was impossible. He'd get $20, and by the next day, it was gone—fast food, gaming skins, you name it. But once he started asking *how* he could make his money last—and looked for ways to save just $2 a day—he started building momentum. A month later, he had his first $60 in savings. That was all it took for his mindset to flip.

It wasn't a miracle. It was a *mindset.*

Embracing Financial Confidence: You Don't Need to Be a Human Calculator

Let me tell you a secret that schools don't always share: **You don't need to be good at math to be good with money**.

Seriously. If you can count change, compare prices, and set a simple goal, you've got what it takes.

Confidence with money isn't about being perfect. It's about taking small steps consistently. One win at a time.

Take Jasmine, for example—a high school student I worked with who thought money "just wasn't her thing." She'd get overwhelmed looking at bank statements and even felt embarrassed asking questions in class. But she started tracking her spending with a notebook—nothing fancy. And after two weeks, she realized she was spending more on snacks than she thought. So, she cut back, saved $10 that month, and her confidence skyrocketed.

That's how it happens. Not with huge wins, but with **small victories that stack**. One good decision becomes two. Two become a habit. And before you know it, you're not just learning about money—you're using it like a pro.

Yet another student, Michael, started with zero confidence and a lot of debt from buying the latest tech on credit. After working through the basics of budgeting, he made a plan, stuck with it, and paid off his first $100. He told me it felt better than buying anything he'd ever splurged on. Why? Because it gave him control.

That's what confidence with money looks like: control, clarity, and calm—even when things get tough.

Let's Recap

- The way you think about money either builds you up or holds you back.
- A **scarcity mindset** says "I can't," while an **abundance mindset** asks "How can I?"
- You don't need to be a math genius to succeed—you just need to believe that you can learn.
- Confidence isn't born. It's **built**, one smart money move at a time.

So, before we talk budgets or savings goals, we've got to get your mindset right. Because when your mind is in the right place, the money starts to follow.

The Dopamine Trap: Why Social Media Is Ruining Your Money Mindset

Let's talk about your brain. More specifically, the part of your brain that gets hijacked every time you see a viral TikTok or a "limited time only" hoodie drop.

That sneaky little brain chemical called *dopamine* is the reason you get hooked. It's the feel-good hit you get when someone likes your post, when you scroll past a funny cat video, or when a package shows up at your door with something you barely remember ordering. Instant reward. Instant pleasure. Zero effort. Your brain *loves it.*

But here's the problem: dopamine isn't just about fun. It's about habits. And when your brain gets used to quick hits, it starts craving more of them. Enter the dopamine trap—a loop where you choose instant gratification (scrolling, spending, swiping) over long-term reward (saving, planning, building).

The Instant Gratification Problem

Let's be real. Saving money doesn't make your phone light up with hearts. Budgeting doesn't have a trendy sound. But binge-watching YouTube Shorts or hitting "buy now" on Amazon? That's easy dopamine.

Social media platforms are *designed* to keep you hooked. Every scroll, like, or swipe is engineered to keep your brain firing off dopamine hits. The same way a slot machine makes gamblers feel alive, your feed makes your brain think you're accomplishing something—even when you're just lying in bed.

The hard truth? Your brain is being trained to love shortcuts. And money success doesn't work that way. It rewards the *opposite.*

Saving for something big. Sticking to a plan. Waiting 24 hours before you spend. These are long-term moves that lead to real growth, real power, real freedom.

It's not as flashy, but it works. And the science backs it: People who delay gratification (like in the famous "marshmallow test") tend to do better in school, careers, and yes, *with money.*

The Danger of Social Media Spending Traps

Now, let's talk about how TikTok, YouTube, and Insta Reels are emptying your wallet faster than you can say "Temu haul."

Ever seen one of those "Amazon Must-Haves You Didn't Know You Needed" videos? Or "Top 5 Tech Gadgets Under $50"?

One teen I worked with—let's call her Mia—saw one of those influencer videos and ended up spending $500 over three months on random viral products. A mini projector she never used. A neon light shaped like a cactus. A milk frother she used twice. Cute? Maybe. Worth it? She didn't think so after checking her bank balance.

Mia told me it felt like her money had evaporated—and that sick feeling stayed with her way longer than the 15 minutes of excitement she got opening the packages.

The point is, brands *know* how to get your attention. They pay influencers to sell you a lifestyle—the idea that if you just buy this one thing, you'll finally feel cool, confident, or complete. But here's the thing: You don't need to buy an aesthetic to be valuable.

Simple Hacks to Outsmart the Trap

- Unfollow or mute accounts that constantly push products.
- Before you buy, ask: *"Would I want this if no one ever saw me with it?"*
- Keep a "wishlist" instead of buying right away. Wait seven days. Still want it? Then maybe it's worth it.

Rewiring Your Brain for Financial Success

Here's the good news: You can absolutely train your brain to crave financial wins the same way it craves that next scroll.

Ever watched your savings account grow a little each week? Hit a money goal? Paid off something small? That *can* be your new dopamine. But it takes practice.

Instead of looking for pleasure in the short term, start looking for satisfaction in progress.

Try these techniques:

- **The 24-Hour Rule**: Want to buy something? Wait a full day. 9 out of 10 times, the urge passes. If not, you'll know it's something you really want.

- **Visual Triggers**: Put a savings tracker on your wall or fridge. Watching your goal inch closer is deeply satisfying.

- **The "Why" Reminder**: Post a sticky note near your phone or computer that says: *"What am I really working toward?"* Seriously. This makes your goals louder than the ads.

Altogether, you're not just building savings. You're building *discipline.* And with that discipline, you're learning to delay short-term dopamine for long-term satisfaction.

And that, right there, is the secret sauce.

Setting Goals: The Secret to Making Money Work for You

Now, let me drop some truth on you that they don't teach you in school: **Money doesn't just work for people who have a lot of it—it works for people who give it a job**.

You wouldn't show up to basketball practice without a coach and expect to win, right? You also wouldn't walk into a kitchen without a recipe and hope to whip up a five-star lasagna (unless you're a chaos wizard). So, why do most people expect to win with their money without ever setting a game plan?

Well, that's where goals come in. Let's break it down.

Dream Big, Start Small

What do you actually want out of life?

Not what your parents want. Not what your friends think is cool. We're talking about *you*, here!

Do you want to save for your first car? Backpack across Europe? Start your own small business selling vintage tees (T-Shirts)? Great. Let's make it happen.

But big dreams require a few baby steps.

Let me introduce you to Harry, a 15-year-old with a dream of going to New York for a teen coding bootcamp.

Total cost? Around **$1,200**.

Harry didn't have rich parents or a trust fund. But what he did have? A plan.

He broke it down:

- $1,200 in 6 months = $200/month
- $200 ÷ 4 weeks = $50/week

He started tutoring a neighbor's kid in math once a week for $20. On Saturdays, he babysat. He even sold two video games he never played. Boom—first week, he hit $50.

Six months later? Harry was in NYC, learning Python and eating dollar pizza under skyscrapers. He didn't just reach his goal—he *earned* it. One week at a time.

Your dream might be different, but the steps are the same. Break it down. Make it real. Then build your plan, one action at a time. Truly, big goals aren't all that intimidating when you slice them into bite-sized wins.

SMART Goals for Money

Now that you've got a dream, let's put it through the SMART filter. No, not "get good grades" smart. I'm talking:

- **S**pecific
- **M**easurable
- **A**ttainable
- **R**elevant
- **T**ime-bound

Let's take two versions of a goal:

1. "I want to save money."
2. "I'm going to save $20 a week from my allowance for the next three months to buy a new phone."

Which one do you think actually gets results? Spoiler: it's the second option.

Here's how to write your own:

- **Specific** – What exactly are you saving for?
- **Measurable** – How much will it cost?
- **Attainable** – Can you realistically save that amount each week?
- **Relevant** – Does this goal matter to you?
- **Time-bound** – When do you want to reach it?

Your turn (grab your notepad):

Write down your **Top 3 Financial Goals** right now. Keep them SMART. Be honest. Be bold. Make Future You proud.

Accountability and Rewards

Let's be honest—setting a goal is easy. Sticking to it, though? That's where most people tap out. But not you. You've got tools.

1. Tell someone

When you tell a friend, parent, or mentor about your goal, it's like putting a little spotlight on it. You're more likely to follow through because someone's watching (not in a creepy way—just a supportive one!).

2. Track your wins visually

Make a savings thermometer. Color in blocks every time you hit a new amount. Or, you could even use an app that celebrates with confetti when you hit a milestone. (We all love digital confetti, don't we?)

3. Celebrate small wins

Saved up your first $50? Do a happy dance. Reached half your goal? Treat yourself to something small and budget-friendly (not the entire sneaker store). Make no mistake, rewards keep your motivation tank full.

Recap

Goals give your money direction. Habits give it speed. Together, they build a future you'll actually want to live.

So, dream big. Start small. Stick with it. And remember, every time you choose to save instead of spend, you're casting a vote for the future you actually want.

How Habits Shape Your Financial Future

Let's pause for a moment and get real. If you walk away from this book and only remember *one thing*, let it be this:

Your habits shape your money future.

Not your grades. Not your allowance. Not how much you know about investing or crypto or "the economy." **Your habits.**

They're like autopilot settings for your life. Once you build a habit, it starts running in the background—without you even thinking about it. Which is both powerful *and* dangerous.

Brushing your teeth? Habit. Unlocking your phone first thing in the morning? Habit. Scrolling TikTok when you're bored? Definitely a habit.

What Is a Habit & How Can You Build One?

A habit is a **repeated action** that eventually becomes automatic. Psychologists break it down into a simple loop:

Cue → Routine → Reward

Let's decode that, *Easy Peasy* style:

- **Cue:** You see or feel something that kicks off the behavior.
- **Routine:** You do the thing.
- **Reward:** You get a result or feeling that reinforces the habit.

Let's say every time you feel stressed (cue), you open up your favorite shopping app and start browsing the latest gadgets (routine), and it gives you a buzz of excitement (reward). *That's* a habit. Your brain files it away as a shortcut: "Feeling bad? Buy something!"

But what if we flipped that?

What if your cue was seeing your allowance hit your account, your routine was setting aside $10 in savings, and your reward was watching your future travel fund grow week by week?

Same loop. *Way* better outcome.

Here's a better visual:

Think about how many times a day you unlock your phone. You don't even think about it—your thumb just *knows* where to go automatically. *That's* a habit. Imagine if saving, budgeting, or making smart money choices felt that natural, too.

That's the goal of this book—to help you build **money habits that run on autopilot** and push you toward success, not away from it.

Noah's Money Tip: You don't need to be perfect. You just need to be *consistent.*

Let me introduce you to Tony.

At 15, Tony was 60 pounds overweight, chronically tired, and deeply uncomfortable in his own skin. PE class? He avoided it like a dentist appointment. Group photos? Forget it. He'd rather disappear than see himself in one.

His daily routine was a recipe for low energy and high regret. School. Chips. Soda. Video Games. Repeat. It wasn't that he didn't care—he just didn't know how to change.

Then one day, during a quiet moment in the school library (aka the only room with working air conditioning and a bully-free zone), Tony picked up a book about habits. He flipped through it half-heartedly, until one page caught his eye:

Cue → Routine → Reward

That's how habits work, it said. Every single one of them.

So Tony started looking at his own loop:

- **Cue**: Get home from school feeling exhausted, stressed, and hungry.
- **Routine**: Open the cupboard, grab chips, crash on the couch, scroll TikTok for an hour.
- **Reward**: A temporary mood boost and a hit of dopamine-fueled comfort.

Sound familiar?

The problem wasn't the cue—school was always going to be tiring. But maybe, just maybe, he could change the routine.

So, he made some swaps:

- Instead of chips, he grabbed a banana with peanut butter.
- Instead of scrolling, he went for a 15-minute walk while listening to music.
- Instead of feeling guilty afterward, he started tracking wins in a notebook.

Same cue. Same need for comfort. But now, a routine that paid off in better energy, more confidence, and eventually serious results.

After two weeks? He felt a bit less sluggish. After a month? His clothes fit better. And by the end of the semester? Tony had dropped 15 pounds, started weight training twice a week, and realized the most important part: *the habit was sticking.* It was becoming automatic. The new normal.

Same cue. New routine. Better reward.

And then something amazing happened: Tony applied that same logic to his money.

He got his first part-time job—bagging groceries on weekends. On payday, the cue was always the same: that rush of excitement when money hit his account. The old routine? Spend it all by Monday on snacks, takeout, and impulse buys.

But now he knew better. He'd paused. He'd ask himself, *What am I really feeling right now?* Then, he'd do something productive with that impulse.

New routine? He transferred $20 straight into savings.

New reward? Watching his money grow and realizing he could actually afford his own phone upgrade without asking his parents.

Tony didn't become a millionaire overnight. But he cracked the code:

Habits aren't about being perfect. They're about building loops that serve you, not sabotage you.

And if he could do it—so can you.

Where This Habit Formula Came From

Okay, real quick—how do we *know* this habit loop even works?

Because a group of Scientists and Researchers at MIT stuck a bunch of lab rats in a maze.

Here's what happened:

- **Cue**: At the start of the maze, the rats heard a "click" sound—this was their signal that a reward was waiting if they made it to the end.

- **Routine**: At first, the rats stumbled around like confused toddlers. But over time, they started remembering the right turns and zoomed through the maze faster and faster.

- **Reward**: At the finish line? Cheese, of course. Their brains lit up like fireworks—because they were *expecting* it.

Here's the interesting part: Scientists scanned the rats' brains during the experiment and found that their decision-making activity actually **decreased** over time.

Why? Because the behavior had become automatic. A *neurological habit loop* was born. Their brains said, "I know this cue. I've got a routine. Let's go get the cheese!"

Later, a journalist named **Charles Duhigg** broke this all down in a bestselling book called *The Power of Habit* (2012), and helped people like us realize:

If rats can build habits that fast… *So can we.*

Duhigg's work demonstrated how powerful this framework is for both breaking bad habits and forming good ones. He applied it to everything from personal finance to business and productivity.

The Cue → Routine → Reward or the CRR loop is literally **how your brain wires habits**—whether it's saving $5, skipping fast food, or building a side hustle that earns you money while you sleep.

Breaking Bad Money Habits

There's no getting around it—bad habits are sneaky. They don't feel dangerous in the moment, but they cost you over time.

Here are a few I see all the time:

- **Impulse spending:** "I've got money—I *deserve* this snack/game/jacket."

- **Procrastination:** "I'll figure out saving later."

- **Avoidance:** "I don't want to look at my balance—it's too low anyway."

These are totally normal, but you know what? They don't serve you. The trick isn't to feel guilty. It's to get *curious.*

Ask yourself:

- "What's triggering this?"
- "What could I do differently?"
- "What's one tiny swap I could try this week?"

That's how we replace bad money habits with intentional ones. For every habit that drains your wallet, there's a better one that can build it.

Bad Habit	**Swap With**
Impulse buys	The "24-hour pause" rule
Ignoring your budget	Weekly money check-in
Feeling broke = giving up	$1/day micro-savings habit

Remember, Tony didn't try to magically "stop being lazy." Instead, he **replaced** one habit loop with a better one. Same boredom. Different routine. Same reward—but healthier, stronger, and more fulfilling.

And you can absolutely do the same.

- **Cue:** You feel bored or stressed.
- **Routine:** Instead of buying something online, write down a money goal.
- **Reward:** A feeling of control and progress (plus, no buyer's remorse).

The Trick to Making Money Habits Stick

Now that we know how habits work, let's talk about **how to make them stick.**

The secret? You stack them. You link them. You build them into the life you *already live.*

This is called **habit stacking**, and it works like magic.

Let's say you already brush your teeth every morning (I hope!). What if, directly before or after brushing, you

- check your budgeting app?
- add a dollar to your savings jar?
- review your "Future Me" goals stuck to the mirror?

Seriously, these things take *less than a minute*, but over time, they change *everything.*

Another tip: Use **visual cues** to keep your habits top-of-mind.

- Put your savings tracker on your wall.
- Keep a sticky note on your laptop that says, *"Pause before you spend."*
- Set a reminder on your phone to reflect every Friday on your wins.

And finally—**give it 30 days.**

That's the golden window. Truly, do something every day for 30 days, and you *will* start to feel the shift.

Why This Chapter Matters (And Why We'll Keep Referring Back to It)

We're calling this "Habit 1" for a reason. Because every chapter after this will be another habit—a new building block on top of the one you just learned.

And every time, we'll come back to this simple truth:

Habits aren't about perfection. They're about repetition.

You don't have to be rich to build great money habits.

You just have to show up—small steps, big vision, every day.

Let this chapter be your launchpad.

Habit 1: Key Chapter Takeaway

- Your mindset is the engine. Your habits are the fuel.
- Where you drive from here? That's 100% your choice.
- Start with one small habit. One small shift. One small win.
- Success isn't about being perfect—it's about building momentum.
- And once you do, there's no limit to where you can go.

So gear up, take the wheel, and ask yourself:

What winning habit will I build next?

Interactive Challenges:

Take Control of Your Money Mindset

Okay, ready to put what you've learned into action? Throughout this book, you'll find fun, interactive challenges, real-world scenarios, and self-assessments to help you build lifelong money habits. The more you participate, the stronger your financial skills will become—so let's dive in!

Part 1: Self-Assessment – How Do You Think About Money?

Choose the statements that best describe you:

- **(A)** I avoid thinking about money because it stresses me out.
- **(B)** I believe I can learn how to manage money and improve over time.
- **(C)** I always feel like I'll never have enough money, no matter what I do.
- **(D)** I get excited when I find ways to save, budget, or invest—even in small amounts.

Reflection: If you chose A or C, your mindset may be holding you back. If you chose B or D, though, you're on the right path to an abundance mindset!

Part 2: Real-Life Scenario – What Would You Do?

Scenario 1

You just got your first paycheck from your part-time job—$250 for two weeks of work. You feel excited to have your own money for the first time!

Your best friend wants you to go to a concert that costs $80, but you also want to start saving for a car. So, what do you do?

Choose one of the following responses:

- **(A)** Spend the money on the concert—you can always save later.
- **(B)** Say no to the concert and put all $250 into savings.
- **(C)** Find a balance—set aside $40 for the concert and $40 for savings.
- **(D)** Look for ways to make extra money so you can do both.

Reflection: Which choice aligns with your long-term goals? What do you think a financially confident person would do?

Part 3: Dopamine Detox Challenge

Challenge: One-Day Dopamine Reset

For the next **24 hours**, challenge yourself to **avoid** instant gratification habits that drain your focus and money. Try this:

✓ **No unnecessary scrolling** on TikTok, Instagram, or YouTube Shorts.

✓ **No impulse spending**—before you buy anything, wait 24 hours.

✓ **Find a long-term reward activity** instead (e.g., add money to savings, learn about investing, or plan a financial goal).

Reflection: How did it feel to resist quick dopamine hits? Did you feel more in control of your time and money?

Part 4: The Habit Challenge – Build One Money Habit This Week

Choose **ONE** money habit below and commit to doing it for **seven days**:

1. The "Future You" Decision Test

Next time you're about to spend some money (snacks, games, clothes, etc.), pause and ask yourself:

- Would my future self thank me for this purchase?
- If I wait 24 hours, will I still want this?
- What would a financially smart person do?
- **Why?** These questions encourage a little mindfulness before spending. They also reinforce the importance of delayed gratification.

2. Start the $1 Savings Habit

- Every day, set aside at least $1 (or a small percentage of your allowance/income).
- Each week, increase it slightly ($1 becomes $2, then $3, etc.).

- **Why?** Saving small amounts consistently builds the habit without feeling overwhelming. And over time, this adds up to *real money*!

3. Dopamine Swap

Every time you feel the urge to scroll through social media or buy something impulsively, swap it with a productive action:

- Read one page of a book.
- Set a money goal.
- Watch an educational video.
- **Why?** Social media tricks your brain into craving instant gratification, but training yourself to enjoy long-term rewards (like growing savings) makes money success feel genuinely exciting.

Reflection:

- Which habit did you choose?
- What was the hardest part of sticking to it?
- Did this habit change the way you think about money?

Part 5: Discussion & Group Activity: Teaching Money Mindset

For Educators, Parents, and Homeschoolers

Task: Lead a **group discussion** (classroom, homeschool, or family setting) about **money beliefs** and how they shape financial decisions.

Discussion agenda:

1. How did your family talk about money when you were younger?

- Was money seen as stressful or exciting?
- Did you ever hear phrases like "money doesn't grow on trees" or "rich people are greedy"?
- How do you think this shaped your mindset about money?

2. **Think about a recent time you made a purchase.**

- What was going through your mind before you bought it?
- Did you feel guilty or excited about spending?
- If you had waited 24 hours, would you still have made the same decision?

3. Reframing the Narrative

- What's the difference between saying, "I can't afford this," and "How can I afford this?"
- How would **a financially smart person** handle this situation differently?
- What's one **practical change** you can make this week to build **better spending habits**?

Activity: The "Money Mindset Jar"

Supplies Needed: A jar, slips of paper, pens

1. Write down one negative money belief you've had (e.g., "I'm just not good with money" or "Money is hard to make").

2. Crumple it up and throw it away!

3. Now, write a new positive money belief to replace it (e.g., "I can learn to manage money well" or "Money is a tool to create opportunities").

4. Place your new belief in the "Money Mindset Jar"—review it daily for one week!

Pro Tip for Teachers & Parents: *Make the* ***Money Mindset Jar*** *a long-term habit! Each month, encourage your students to* ***write a new financial belief they've learned*** *and replace an old one. Over time, they'll* ***see how their mindset grows!***

Action Habit 1: Train Your Brain for Financial Success

The Habit:

Every time you catch yourself thinking, *"I can't afford this,"* reframe it to: *"How can I afford this?"*

Daily Action:

Whenever you want something (new clothes, gaming console, concert ticket, etc.), ask yourself:

1. "How can I make this happen?"
2. "What would a financially smart person do?"
3. "Do I need to buy this now, or can I wait?"

Why It Works:

- This shifts you from a scarcity mindset to an abundance mindset.

- You train your brain to look for solutions instead of roadblocks.
- Over time, you start seeing opportunities instead of limitations.

✓ **Challenge:** Try this for seven days and track how often you change your mindset. Notice how it affects your decisions!

Habit 1 Progress Check: Did You Take Action?

✓ Quick Review

- Did you complete the **Self-Assessment** on your money mindset?
- Did you do the **24-Hour Dopamine Detox Challenge**?
- Did you participate in a **Discussion or Activity** about money mindset?

✓ Rate Your Progress (1–5 Stars)

★ ★ ★ ★ ★ *(How well did you apply today's lessons?)*

Ready to Move On? *Great work! Before moving on, though, take a moment to reflect:*

- What was your biggest takeaway?
- **How has your mindset about money changed?**

Why not discuss your thoughts with a friend, family member, or teacher? Then, when you're ready, dive into the next chapter to continue mastering your money mindset!

Habit 2:

Mastering Budgeting: The Blueprint for Financial Freedom

A budget isn't a restriction—it's your permission slip to spend smarter and live better.

Think of it like this:

A budget isn't a boring list of things you *can't* do.

It's your **game plan** to do the things you actually *want* to do, without waking up broke and panicked the next morning.

What Is a Budget?

The Purpose of Budgeting

Let's start easy:

A **budget** is just **a plan for your money**.

No spreadsheets. No Wall Street vibes. No brain-melting math.

It's literally you telling your dollars where to go **before** they run off on their own. Think about it like this:

You wouldn't plan a road trip without Google Maps, right? Otherwise, you'd just be driving in circles, burning gas, and hoping you magically end up at the beach. Well, same goes with money. No plan equals no destination. Got it?

Why Budgets = Control

When you budget, you're in charge. You're telling your money,

- "You're going toward my car savings."
- "You're buying me those concert tickets next month."
- "You're helping Future Me move out at 18."

So, instead of wondering where it all went, you know exactly where it's *going.*

Mini Test

If you got $100 today, could you immediately say what you would spend/save it on? (If your answer is "Uh... snacks?", you need a budget, my friend.)

Why Budgeting Gives You More Freedom, Not Less

Most people think budgeting feels like putting themselves on lockdown. No fun. No treats. No joy.

Well, guess what? Most people are wrong.

Budgeting gives you the freedom to **spend without guilt**. See, when you *plan* for fun, you *enjoy* the fun.

- You can buy that new hoodie or beanie—because you planned for it.
- You can go to that movie night—because it's already in your budget.
- You can save for your first car—without feeling like you have to live like a monk.

In short, planning equals permission, not punishment.

Real-Life Teen Example: Tyler and the $500 Bike

Let's talk about **Tyler**. What can I tell you about this kid? He was 14 years old, and he *really* wanted a new mountain bike for the summer. The price tag of his dream bike, though? *$500.*

His allowance? $100 a month (if he mowed the lawn without whining, that is). At first, he thought, "No way. That's too much."

But then, he made a budget:

- $100 income
- $20 for snacks and hanging out with friends
- $80 to put straight into his "Bike Fund"

Month by month, it grew:

$80... $160... $240... (you get the picture).

After six months, he had enough cash to walk into the bike shop, slap his money down, and ride out to freedom.

No debt. No begging parents. No random "How did I spend $100 on candy?!" regret. Just a goal, a plan, and the flex of buying it *himself.*

Quick Reflection

If you had $500 right now, what would *you* save for? (Pause. Think about it. Write it down somewhere.)

The 50/30/20 Rule Made Simple

Alright, let's make budgeting even **easier** with one of my favorite formulas:

The 50/30/20 Rule

Here's the deal:

- **50%** → Needs (stuff you must pay for—like lunch money, phone bill, transportation)
- **30%** → Wants (stuff you love—concerts, apps, snacks, fashion)
- **20%** → Savings (your future cash vault)

Super simple, super flexible.

Adjusting for Teens With Limited Income

Look, I get it—you're not paying rent or buying groceries yet (hopefully). But you still have *mini* "needs" and "wants."

Example:

Let's say you get **$200** a month from part-time work. Here's how you could split it:

- $100 (50%) → Your "needs" like school lunches, transportation, or helping with bills
- $60 (30%) → Your "wants"—new games, hanging out with friends

- $40 (20%) → Savings for your big goal (new laptop, car, whatever)

Easy math. Even easier freedom.

Quick Micro-Test

You just earned $50.

According to the 50/30/20 rule, how much should you save? (Hint: 20% of $50 = ?)

(Answer: **$10** into savings! Nice.)

Common Budgeting Myths (And Why They're Trash)

Okay, before going any further, let's take a moment to bust some budgeting myths.

Myth 1: "I Don't Have Enough Money to Budget"

Truth: Budgeting is *especially* important when you don't have much. Small budgets equal a bigger need for a plan. (Just ask Tyler and his bike fund!)

Myth 2: "Budgeting Takes Too Much Time"

Truth: It takes 10 minutes a week.

Literally. You can set a timer and budget during a commercial break. (Or... three TikToks. Depends on how you measure your life.)

Myth 3: "I Can't Have Fun If I Budget"

Truth: Budgeting **bakes fun into the plan**, so you enjoy it without blowing everything.

- Budget for fun.
- Spend guilt-free.
- Repeat.

Reflection

What feels scarier:

- Having a plan for your money?
- Or having no idea where it all disappeared? (I know what Future You would say!)

Creating Your First Teen-Friendly Budget

Alright, you've got the basics down—what a budget is, why it matters, and how it can actually *free* you instead of trap you. Now, then, it's time for the fun part: building your very first teen-friendly budget!

Don't worry—this isn't some boring spreadsheet nightmare. It's about designing a simple, flexible plan that makes your money work *for* you, not *against* you.

Let's get into it.

Tracking Your Spending: Find Out Where Your Money's Actually Going

First things first—you can't create a budget if you don't know where your money is slipping away.

So, this week, I want you to track *every single dollar* you spend. Yes, even that $2.99 boba tea.

Here's your mini mission:

Easy Peasy Action Step

- Grab a notepad, open your notes app, or better yet—use the free Monthly Budget Planner that comes with this book (just scan the QR code!).
- For the next seven days, **write down everything you spend money on**. Every snack. Every online order. Every gas station slushie. Again, no judgment here—just data.

Why?

Because most teens (and let's be honest, most adults) think they know where their money's going—but once they track it, they're shocked.

You can even use free budgeting apps like:

- **YNAB (You Need a Budget)**
- **Mint**
- **PocketGuard**

(We'll talk more about budgeting apps later—but for now, just focus on seeing where your money leaks!)

Mini Reality Check

"I thought I was just buying a few snacks a week... turns out I spent $38 on chips, sodas, and McFlurries this *month!"*—real teen, real budget wake-up call.

When you track every dollar, you get the full picture. And *only then* can you start making choices that actually line up with your goals.

Real Teen Example

My student Ethan started tracking every dollar he spent using PocketGuard. At first, he was shocked to see how much was disappearing due to energy drinks and game upgrades. But by cutting back just a little each week—and seeing it all clearly—he managed to save over $200 in three months without feeling deprived. *That's* the power of awareness!

Quick Check-In

Where do you think most of your money leaks out? Snacks? Online shopping? Subscriptions? Make a quick guess now, then compare it after seven days of tracking. You might be surprised!

Setting Up Your Budget Categories: Make It Yours

So, now that you know where your cash is disappearing, it's time to organize it into **budget categories**.

Here are some typical ones for teens:

- eating out /snacks
- entertainment (movies, gaming subscriptions, streaming platforms)
- clothing/fashion

- transport (bus pass, gas money, Uber)
- phone/internet
- school supplies
- savings (yes, it gets its own category!)

Easy Peasy Tip: Always include a **Fun Fund!**

Saving is important, but so is living your life. Budget a little for "fun money" so you're not miserable.

Example Time

Let's say you have $300/month from a part-time job:

- $50 for food/snacks
- $40 for entertainment
- $30 for clothing
- $50 for transportation
- $80 into savings
- $30 for your phone bill
- $20 Fun Fund

Notice how savings isn't the *leftover*—it's the *priority*. Smart money moves.

(And psst—again, if you want an even easier way to set this up, grab the **Monthly Budget Planner Printable** or **Spreadsheet** included free with your book. It'll lay it all out for you in a super simple way!)

Adjusting and Sticking to Your Budget: Flex, Don't Stress

Here's the honest truth:

Your first budget will probably be a little messy.

You might forget something (hello, birthday gift for your cousin!). Or you might overspend on movie snacks. It's *normal.*

The key?

Review and tweak your budget every month.

Ask yourself:

- "Where did I overspend?"
- "Where did I underspend?"
- "What can I adjust for next month?"

When it comes down to it, budgeting isn't about being perfect. It's about being *aware.* It's like steering a car—you're always making tiny corrections to stay on course.

Bonus Tip

When you stick to your budget for the month—even if it's not perfect—**reward yourself.** Seriously.

Got $20 left over? Maybe treat yourself to a coffee date or a new journal. Don't go overboard, but it's so important to take a second to celebrate those smart money wins of yours!

Mini Reflection

Before you move on, answer this quick question:

"What's one category I usually overspend on—and what's one small change I could make next month?"

Write it down. Even tiny changes make a big difference over time.

Quick Recap

- Track every dollar for a week—know your spending habits cold.
- Set realistic budget categories—including savings and fun.
- Adjust every month—flexibility is your secret weapon.

I'll say it again: Budgeting isn't about being perfect. It's about building *awareness* and *confidence.* And if you ever feel overwhelmed?

Just remember—you're not alone.

You've got this guide. You've got your bonuses.

And you've got the power to take control of your money—one *Easy Peasy* step at a time.

Staying on Track: How to Keep Your Budget Game Strong

Alright—you've built your first budget. You're feeling like a money ninja. You're about to dominate your finances and retire at 30.

But wait.

Now comes the real test: **sticking to it.**

Don't worry—this *also* isn't about being perfect. It's about knowing the curveballs coming your way and having a few moves ready to dodge them.

First off, let's dive into some of the strategies that will keep you winning long after the excitement of your first budget wears off.

Overcoming Budget Busters

I'm sorry to say, but even the best budgets get punched in the face sometimes. Here's how to spot the troublemakers and handle them like a pro:

Common Pitfall 1: Overspending on Food and Entertainment

Ask any teen (or any human being, really) where their money leaks out, and it's almost always snacks, gaming, Uber Eats, and late-night Amazon browsing.

True story: I once had a student, Jake, who thought he was "doing fine" until he tracked his spending and realized he had spent $140—yes, *$140*—on boba tea and movie tickets in just two months. And he didn't even like half the movies!

Easy Peasy Fix:

Set yourself a spending limit in your fun categories ahead of time.

For example:

- $30/month for snacks
- $40/month for entertainment

And if you hit your limit early, don't panic—just hit pause until next month. It's not about saying no to fun forever. It's just about setting boundaries that your future self will actually thank you for!

Common Pitfall 2: Saying Yes to Every Friend Invite

You've got your budget all mapped out, and then your friends hit you with, "*Hey, we're all grabbing food after school. You're coming, right?*"

Cue the guilt trip.

Easy Peasy Fix:

Have a simple go-to line ready:

- "*I'm saving for something big right now, but I'll definitely catch up next time!*"
- Or suggest a cheaper alternative: "*I'm down for hanging out, but can we do something free like chill at the park or do a movie night at someone's place?*"

Most real friends won't care if you're smart with your money. And if they do? That says more about them than about you.

Common Pitfall 3: Life Changes = Budget Changes

New job? New expenses? Surprise field trip fee?

Your budget isn't carved into stone like an ancient Egyptian tablet. It's a living thing that needs updates.

Easy Peasy Tip:

Every time something big shifts—new income, new goals, unexpected expenses—do a quick 10-minute "budget tune-up."

It's like updating your GPS after a wrong turn. You don't ditch the car—you just reroute!

Remember Tony?

Our boy Tony (from Chapter 1) didn't just lose weight by accident. He recognized his triggers (cue), swapped his routine, and chased better rewards. Budgeting works the same way.

If you get off track one month (overspending, unexpected costs, etc.), don't freak out. Just adjust your routine. The goal isn't to be perfect—it's to keep moving forward.

Creating a Zero-Based Budget: Give Every Dollar a Job

Here's a budgeting trick that sounds a little complicated but is actually ridiculously simple—and powerful:

Zero-based budgeting

It means:

Income - Expenses = Zero

In other words, every single dollar you earn has a mission. A job. A *purpose.*

No dollar left sitting around getting bored (because bored dollars tend to wander off and buy hoodies you don't need).

How It Works

Let's say you earn $300 a month from your part-time job. You could plan it like this:

Category	Amount
Food and Snacks	$40
Entertainment	$30

Transportation	$50
Clothing	$20
Savings	$100
Fun Fund	$30
School Supplies	$30
TOTAL	**$300**

See that? Every dollar is accounted for. No loose change. No "where did my money go?" moments.

Mini Reflection

Ask yourself: "If I gave every dollar a job right now, what's one thing I would prioritize that I usually forget?"

Write it down—it'll make a huge difference next month.

Quick Tip

You can grab the free *Monthly Budget Planner* that comes with this book (QR code inside!) to create your own zero-based budget easily.

Staying Motivated to Budget

Budgeting is a marathon, not a sprint. With that in mind, motivation is bound to dip sometimes. And that's completely normal. So, here's how to keep your energy high without turning into a financial robot:

1. Turn It Into a Game

Challenge yourself each month:

- Can you save $10 more than last month?
- Can you spend $20 less on snacks without feeling deprived?

Gamify it. Make it fun. Even create "budget battles" with a sibling or friend to see who can hit their goals faster.

2. Use Visual Trackers

Humans are visual creatures. We love seeing progress.

- Make a savings thermometer that you color in every time you hit a goal.
- Create a sticker chart on your wall.
- Use an app that throws digital confetti when you save money. (Yes, even teens like confetti. It's *science*.)

3. Try the "Cash Envelope" Method

Old-school but crazy effective:

Take your budgeted money for a category (like snacks or entertainment) out in cash and put it in an envelope.

When the envelope's empty? That's it for the month!

It's like giving yourself built-in guardrails—without relying on willpower alone.

Quick Recap

- Budget busters happen—plan ahead for them.
- Zero-based budgeting = every dollar has a mission.

- Keep your motivation alive with games, trackers, and smart hacks.
- Remember Tony: slip-ups aren't failures. They're opportunities to swap in better habits.

Habit 2: Key Chapter Takeaway

Remember Tony's story from Habit 1? His real transformation started when he understood the simple CRR habit loop: Cue → Routine → Reward.

Budgeting works the exact same way.

- **Cue:** Every time you get paid (allowance, paycheck, gift).
- **Routine:** Before spending anything, you sit down for five minutes to update your budget using your printable or spreadsheet planner from this book.
- **Reward:** You feel a burst of confidence seeing your savings grow and your goals getting closer.

It's one simple cue → routine → reward loop!

Why is this important? Because when you build the habit of budgeting early, you take control of your money before it has a chance to control you! Over time, budgeting becomes automatic—like brushing your teeth or grabbing your backpack before school—and managing your money starts to feel easy, natural, and empowering.

Small habits create big results. Start your budgeting habit now, and your future self will thank you for it.

Interactive Challenges:

Take Control of Your Budget

Part 1: Self-Assessment – What's Your Budgeting Style?

Choose the statement that best describes you:

- **(A)** "I don't budget—I just spend until my money runs out."
- **(B)** "I try to budget, but I usually forget to track my expenses."
- **(C)** "I budget sometimes but have a hard time sticking to it."
- **(D)** "I plan my spending, track it, and adjust when needed."

Reflection: If you picked A or B, this chapter will help you take control. If you picked C or D, you're on your way—let's fine-tune your skills!

Part 2: Real-Life Scenario – What Would You Do?

Scenario 2

You just received another paycheck—$250 for two weeks of work. You've been wanting to buy a new pair of shoes that cost $150, but you also need money for gas, food, and fun with friends. What's your move?

Choose one:

- **(A)** Buy the shoes immediately—you earned it!
- **(B)** Stick to a budget: allocate money for shoes, savings, and expenses.

- **(C)** Wait a week before buying—see if you still want them.
- **(D)** Find a way to make extra money so you can afford everything.

Reflection: What choice best supports your long-term financial goals?

Part 3: Budget Challenge – Track Your Spending for One Week

Challenge

- For the next seven days, track every dollar you spend—write it down or use a budgeting app.
- At the end of the week, review your spending. Did anything surprise you?

Reflection: What's one thing you could cut back on to save more?

Part 4: The Habit Challenge – Build One Budget Habit This Week

Choose **ONE** budget habit below and commit to doing it for seven days:

1. The "$10 Rule" Challenge

- Before buying something nonessential, wait 10 hours if it's under $10, or 10 days if it's over $100, before purchasing.
- If you still want it after the waiting period, go for it! If not, you just saved money.

- **Why?** This prevents impulse buys and makes sure you're spending on things you truly value.

2. Reverse Budgeting – Pay Yourself First

- Every time you get money (allowance, paycheck, gift, etc.), immediately set aside at least 10% for savings before spending anything.
- **Why?** You make saving a priority instead of an afterthought.

3. The "Cash-Only" Experiment

- For **one week**, take out a set amount of cash for fun spending (e.g., food, entertainment) and **only spend what's in your wallet**.
- No debit/credit cards. No digital payments.
- **Why?** You become more conscious of your spending when you physically see your money disappearing.

Reflection:

- Which habit did you choose?
- What was the hardest part of sticking to it?
- Did it change how you think about budgeting?

Part 5: Discussion & Group Activity – Mastering Budgeting

For Educators, Parents, and Homeschoolers

In this section, educators and parents will guide teens through **real-world budgeting scenarios**, **critical thinking exercises**, and **interactive discussions** to help them develop lifelong budgeting skills in a fun and relatable way!

Discussion: "Where Did My Money Go?"

Goal: Help teens recognize spending patterns, common money drains, and how budgeting can prevent financial stress.

Discussion agenda:

1. Think about the last time you ran out of money.

- What did you spend it on?
- Looking back, do you wish you had planned your spending differently?

2. Have you ever regretted a purchase?

- What was it, and why did you regret it?
- How could a budget have helped prevent this?

3. Imagine you just got $300 as a paycheck or allowance.

- Without looking, guess how much of that would go toward essentials, fun, and savings.
- Now, break it down: How would a well-planned budget change your spending?

Takeaway: Many people don't realize where their money goes until it's gone. A budget **gives you control, not restrictions**—it helps you afford the things that actually matter!

Activity: "The Real Cost of Small Spending"

Supplies Needed: Calculator, pen, and paper (or budgeting app)

Instructions:

- **Step 1:** Ask teens to list three things they buy often (e.g., coffee, snacks, game add-ons, Uber rides).
- **Step 2:** Estimate how much they spend on each per week.
- **Step 3:** Multiply by **four weeks** for a monthly total.
- **Step 4:** Multiply by **12 months** for a yearly total.

Example Calculation:

Takeout food: $10 per week → $40 per month → **$480 per year!**

Game add-ons: $5 per week → $20 per month → **$240 per year!**

Coffee shop visits: $6 per day (x3 per week) → $72 per month → **$864 per year!**

Discussion:

- Were you surprised by how much small purchases add up over time?
- What else could you do with that money? (Save for a trip, invest, buy something meaningful?)
- If you cut one expense in half, how much would you save?

Takeaway: Small, **everyday expenses add up fast**! Budgeting helps you **prioritize spending** on things that truly matter.

Action Habit 2: Become a Budget Boss

The Habit:

Before making a purchase, ask yourself **three quick questions:**

1. Do I *need* this or just *want* it?

2. If I buy this now, will I still have money for my other goals?

3. Could I find a cheaper or smarter way to get it?

Daily Action:

Every time you want to spend money, pause and go through these questions. Trust me, you'll start making smarter choices without feeling restricted.

Why It Works:

- It helps you **avoid impulse spending** and stay on track.

- It teaches **mindful spending**—you're in control of your money, not the other way around!

- Over time, this builds **financial confidence** and smarter money habits.

✓ **Challenge:** Try this for seven days. Notice how it changes the way you spend!

Bonus Challenge: The 30-Day Budget Momentum Challenge

If you're ready to take your budgeting skills to the next level—and seriously build money habits that stick—then this challenge is definitely for you.

You've already done the warm-up with the weekly budgeting challenges. So now? It's time for the real deal: mastering your money for *a full month.*

Here's the mission (should you choose to accept it):

The 30-Day Budget Momentum Challenge

1. **Track every dollar you spend** for the next 30 days. (Use the printable or spreadsheet bonus you downloaded, or just a notebook if you prefer.)

2. **Create your first full budget** using zero-based budgeting. Assign every dollar a job—even if it's just $5 for snacks.

3. **Pick ONE goal** to focus on.

Example: Save $100 for a concert, or spend $50 less on takeout.

4. **Do a weekly check-in** every Sunday.

    - What went right?
    - Where did I slip up?
    - What can I tweak for next week?

5. **Celebrate small wins.**

Hit your goal? Great! Treat yourself (again, within budget) to something meaningful—a book, a pizza night, a day out with friends.

Because celebrating progress is a key part of building momentum!

Why Take This Bonus Challenge?

The thing is, building a budget habit isn't just about one good week—it's about showing Future You that you're capable of sticking to something powerful.

If you can manage your money for 30 days, you can manage it for life. Small habits → Big confidence → Major success.

And once you complete this challenge, budgeting won't feel like a "chore" anymore. It'll feel like second nature—your brain's new default setting for money success!

Habit 2 Progress Check: Did You Take Action?

✓ Quick Review

- Did you complete the Self-Assessment on your budgeting style?
- Did you track your spending for one week?
- Did you complete the **$10 Rule Challenge**, **Reverse Budgeting**, or **Cash-Only Experiment**?

✓ Rate Your Progress (1–5 Stars)

★ ★ ★ ★ ★ *(How well did you apply today's lesson?)*

Next Step:

Ready to move on? Great work! Before moving on, though, take a moment to think about what you've learned:

- **What was your biggest budgeting takeaway?**

- **What's one spending habit you'd like to improve?**
- **Discuss your thoughts with a friend, family member, or teacher!**

Then, when you're all set, flip on over to the next chapter and let's continue mastering your money habits!

Habit 3:

Saving Money the Easy Peasy Way

Every dollar you save today is like planting a seed that grows into a tree full of money tomorrow.

Why Saving Matters

Alright, let's get real.

Saving money isn't just some boring "adult thing" your parents nag you about. It's the secret move that gives you options, freedom, and—let's be honest—some *serious* flex later on.

Think of saving like planting seeds. Tiny at first. Barely noticeable. But over time? Those seeds grow into full-blown money trees. (And who doesn't want a money tree?)

Let's break it down, *Easy Peasy* style.

The Power of Saving Early

Here's a simple truth that most people don't figure out until they're way older (and kinda wish they had):

The earlier you start saving, the easier it is to build real wealth. Small amounts lead to big results over time.

Example

If you save just **$5 a week**, that's **$260** a year.

Now, let's say you also toss that money into a basic savings account that pays you a little bit of interest. (Nothing crazy—even 2% helps.) Over time, your money **grows on its own**. This magical growth is called **compound interest**.

Quick Compound Interest Breakdown

- You earn interest not just on your original money, but also on the interest you've already earned.
- It's like your money having little money babies that grow up and have their own money babies.

Visual: Imagine a snowball rolling downhill. At first, it's tiny. But as it keeps rolling, it collects more snow… and more… until it becomes *huge*.

That's what happens when you save early. Even a few bucks builds massive momentum over time.

Real Teen Story: Meet Kayla

Kayla, 15, started saving $10 a week from babysitting. No big deal, right? But she stuck with it. No excuses.

By the end of one year? **$520.**

And that wasn't even counting extra birthday money, holiday gifts, or little side hustles she picked up along the way.

When a chance to take a dream summer trip popped up, guess what?

Kayla was ready. Paid for her ticket *herself*. No begging. No debt. Just pure "I'm a boss" vibes.

Quick Reflection

What's one thing you'd love to save for right now? Write it down. (Dreams + a plan = unstoppable.)

Emergency Funds for Teens

Yeah, yeah, I know—"emergencies" sound like stuff only grown-ups deal with. But here's the deal: Even teens hit bumps in the road.

Maybe your phone breaks. Maybe you need last-minute cash for a school trip. Maybe your car (if you're lucky enough to have one) needs a random repair.

Having an emergency fund is your "In Case of Life Being Annoying" safety net.

Easy Peasy Target

- First Goal: Save **$100**.
- Next Goal: Grow it to **$500**.

You don't need to do it overnight. It's a slow build. But every $5, every $10 you stash makes you stronger.

Quick quiz time!

What counts as an emergency?

- (A) You get ketchup on your white shirt.
- (B) The Xbox you've wanted is now on sale.
- (C) You crack your phone screen.

Answer: C.

Emergencies are about **needs** you couldn't predict—not "wants" that pop up because you saw a 24-hour flash sale.

Saving for emergencies = future you being calm, not panicked.

Short-Term vs. Long-Term Savings

Saving isn't "one size fits all." Different goals = different timelines.

Short-Term Savings

- concert tickets
- a new bike
- upgrading your laptop

Long-Term Savings

- buying your first car
- moving out after graduation
- starting your own business someday

Easy Peasy Tip: You don't have to choose *either/or*. You can save for both at the same time!

Example: You earn $200 this month. Split your savings like this:

- $100 toward your long-term goal (like "First Car Fund")
- $100 toward short-term goals (like "Concert With Friends Fund")

See? Smart and balanced.

Quick Check-In:

- Name one short-term goal you want to save for.
- Name one long-term goal you want to save for.

Write them down—and let's start growing those money trees!

How to Save More Money

You've got your "*why*" for saving.

Now, let's talk about the "*how*"—in ways that are smart, simple, and—let's be honest—actually doable when you're a busy teen.

Because here's the truth:

Saving money doesn't have to mean living like a medieval monk eating canned beans.

It's about making tiny smart moves that stack up into big results over time. With me so far? Let's keep going.

Automating Savings: Set It and Forget It

One of the best saving hacks of all time is so simple it almost feels like cheating: **Automation**.

Here's how it works:

- Set up a savings account (or use an app like Greenlight).
- Set it to automatically transfer money every week or every time you get paid.
- Done. No thinking. No forgetting. No "oops, I spent it all" moments.

This is called "paying yourself first."

You save before you spend, not after.

Why Automation Works

When you automate saving,

- you don't have to rely on willpower (which is flaky at best).
- you don't miss what you never see in your checking account.
- you build wealth without even trying.

Example

Let's say you automate saving just $10 a week. That's $40 a month.

After one year? $480.

And the best part? You barely even notice it.

Quick Tip

If you've got the printable or spreadsheet bonus with this book (hint: scan the QR code if you haven't!), you can use it to set your first automated saving goal today! *Easy peasy.*

Cutting Costs Without Cutting Fun

Saving doesn't mean you have to give up on having a life. You just have to be *smarter* about it.

How to Save Without Feeling Miserable

- **Switch to Affordable Subscriptions:**

  Instead of three separate streaming services, split one with your family or friends. (Hello, Spotify family plan!)

- **DIY Gifts and Decor:**

  Instead of buying $30 candles and birthday cards, why not learn a few easy DIY skills? Homemade stuff is often way cooler anyway—and way cheaper, to boot.

- **Save on Food:**

  Food is a massive money leak for teens. Instead of Uber Eats three times a week, try

  - planning a "treat day" once a week.
  - packing snacks from home.
  - learning three easy meals you can make yourself for half the cost. (Egg sandwich, anyone?)

- **Save on Shopping:**

  Before you buy something, check for discounts, coupons, or secondhand versions. Apps like Honey or Rakuten can save you money automatically while you shop.

- **Entertainment Hacks:**

  Swap expensive outings for cheaper or free fun:

  - free concerts
  - game nights at home
  - movie nights with friends (pop your own popcorn!)

Quick Reflection

What's one fun thing you love that could cost half as much with a little creativity? Write it down—and challenge yourself to try it next month!

Earning Interest on Your Savings

Now let's get real next-level:

Let your money make more money.

Sounds like magic, right? It's actually just... **interest.**

When you put money into a savings account (especially a high-yield one), the bank **pays you** a little extra just for leaving it there.

Over time, that "little extra" grows bigger and bigger—and that's where **compound interest** kicks in.

Simple Example

- You save $500 in a high-yield savings account.
- It earns about 5% interest each year (if you choose a good one!).
- In five years, with no extra effort, your $500 turns into about **$638**.
- And if you keep adding a little each month? Yup—it grows even faster.

Why Teens Should Avoid "Dead" Cash

Keeping all your money in cash (or even a basic checking account) doesn't help it grow. It just sits there... bored... losing value slowly over time thanks to inflation.

Instead, you want your savings working for you—even while you sleep.

Think of your savings account like planting a tree:

- Plant it once (deposit your money).
- Water it a little (add small savings).
- Watch it grow (earn interest).

A Quick Friendly Note

We know that in some cultures and religions, earning interest isn't always encouraged. If that's you, no worries—you can still grow your money by:

- saving consistently.
- investing in ways that match your values.
- focusing on building assets and financial habits without relying on interest.

Everyone's financial journey can look a little different—and that's totally fine.

Quick Recap: Saving Smarter, Not Harder

- **Automate it—**so saving happens without thinking.
- **Cut costs creatively—**so you save without missing out on life.
- **Let your money grow—**so Future You has way more options.

Staying Motivated to Save

Starting to save money is exciting, isn't it?. How about staying motivated to keep saving? Still exciting? Eh, actually, that's a whole different game. Let's talk about it.

Visualizing Your Goals

I'm going to venture a guess that your brain likes pictures more than boring old lists, yes? It's science, after all (and common sense!). So, let's do a little visualization exercise.

- **Use a Savings Tracker:**

Draw a thermometer, a progress bar, or a mountain you climb every time you add money.

- **Create a Vision Board:**

Cut up some magazines, print out some pics, or use Canva.

What you want to do is make a poster that showcases what you're saving for: your first car, your first solo trip, your first "I'm-so-independent" apartment, and so on.

- **Printable Bonus:**

If you nabbed that free Monthly Budget Planner from earlier, you'll find some easy savings trackers in there that can work superbly here! Don't just use them—decorate them, and own them.

Quick Mission

Right now—yes, literally right this second—think of *one* thing you're saving for and sketch a rough tracker for it. (Ugly drawings still count. Consider them progress!)

The $5 Challenge

Here's a game that's so simple it feels like stealing from yourself (in a good way):

The $5 Challenge.

How it works:

- Every time you get a $5 bill, don't spend it.
- Instead? Stash it. In a jar, envelope, sock drawer, whatever.
- After three months, check how much you secretly saved up.

True Story

One of my students, Stacey, did this challenge without telling anyone. She kept stuffing $5 bills into a shoebox under her bed.

After 90 days?

She had **$275** saved—I'm not kidding. And know what she said? Along the way, she barely missed any of it.

That's the power of tiny habits stacking up.

Bonus Tip

Now, if you're more of a card swiper, you can do a digital version of this same challenge: Every time you spend money, transfer $5 to your savings immediately. It's like a mini penalty... for being *awesome.*

The 24-Hour Rule for Spending

Harsh truth time: Impulse spending? It's the enemy of savings. Sorry, not sorry.

Here's your shield against it:

The 24-Hour Rule

- If something costs more than $20, you can't buy it *today*.
- You have to wait at least 24 hours.

This tiny pause gives your brain time to ask:

- "Do I *really* want this?"
- "Is it worth slowing down my goals for?"
- "Would Future Me thank me or roast me for this?"

Real-Life Trick

Half the time, after 24 hours, you'll forget you even wanted it.

(Shoutout to my almost-purchased, neon green Rollerblades. No regrets.)

Saving isn't just about saying *no* to stuff. It's about saying *yes* to the stuff you actually care about.

Let's Tie It All Together: Building a Saving Habit

Remember Tony from Habit 1? Our dude who learned how to build habits to crush his goals?

He didn't magically wake up one morning good at saving. He built it the same way he built better fitness and budgeting habits—by following the golden CRR formula:

Cue → Routine → Reward

Here's how it works for saving:

- **Cue:** You get money (allowance, paycheck, birthday cash).
- **Routine:** Before spending anything, you put a chunk into savings *first* (even $5).
- **Reward:** You watch your savings tracker grow—or get closer to your goal.

Every time you follow that loop, your brain gets a hit of success.

It feels good. It builds momentum. And over time? **Saving becomes your default mode, not a struggle.**

Why Building a Saving Habit Early Matters

- You train your brain that money isn't just for spending—it's for *building*.
- You grow confidence knowing you can hit goals without freaking out.
- You unlock options, choices, and freedoms that most people *wish* they had.

So, altogether? Saving is your weapon against money stress later. And right now, you're sharpening it into a bona fide superpower.

Small moves → Massive wins over time. That's the *Easy Peasy Way*.

Quick Recap: Keep Saving, Keep Winning

- Make your goals visual so you stay pumped.
- Try the $5 Challenge to sneak-save some serious cash.
- Use the 24-Hour Rule to block impulse buys.

- Lock in the Cue → Routine → Reward (CRR) habit loop for saving like a champ.

It's simple: You've got the tools. You've got the plan.

Now, it's time to build your money tree—one seed at a time. Future You is already nodding in approval.

Habit 3: Key Chapter Takeaway: How Small Saves Create Big Wins

Saving money isn't just about stacking cash like a dragon hoarding gold.

It's about building a life where you get to say "yes" to the things that truly matter—without panic, without debt, and without having to text your parents for emergency money.

By now, you've learned three crucial saving skills:

- Why saving early—even just $5 a week—can turn into thousands over time.

- How setting up an emergency fund protects you from the "oh no" moments of life.

- How to balance saving for short-term wins (like concerts) and long-term dreams (like your first car).

But here's the real secret:

Saving isn't just a one-time decision. It's a habit you build.

You already know the CRR formula: **Cue → Routine → Reward**.

The bigger reason this matters?

Because the earlier you build the saving habit, the easier everything else gets later.

Financial freedom isn't one huge leap—it's a thousand tiny $5 choices that snowball into serious independence.

Final Challenge Before Moving On

- Pick one savings goal right now (small or big—doesn't matter).
- Set your cue (like: "Every payday, I save first. Period.").
- Build the routine.
- Celebrate the reward.

Because saving isn't just about money. It's about freedom, confidence and building the future you actually want, one easy peasy win at a time.

Interactive Challenges:

Take Control of Your Savings

Part 1: Self-Assessment – What Type of Saver Are You?

Choose the statement that best describes you:

- **(A)** "I spend most of my money and rarely save."
- **(B)** "I try to save, but I always end up using my savings."
- **(C)** "I save when I remember, but I don't have a system."
- **(D)** "I have a solid savings plan and stick to it."

Reflection: If you chose A or B, this chapter will help you build a solid savings habit. However, if you chose C or D, you're on the right track—let's take it to the next level!

Part 2: Real-Life Scenario – What Would You Do?

Scenario 3

Your birthday just passed, and your family gave you $300 as a gift. You've been wanting to buy a pair of the latest AirPods, which cost $250, but you also have a long-term goal of saving up for a car.

Choose one:

- **(A)** Buy the AirPods immediately— you've waited long enough!
- **(B)** Put the entire $300 into savings— you can buy the AirPods later if you still want them.
- **(C)** Split the money: save $200, spend $100 on something fun.
- **(D)** Find a way to make extra money so you can afford both.

Reflection: What choice best aligns with your long-term savings goals? How would a financially smart person approach this decision?

Part 3: Savings Challenge – The Seven-Day Savings Boost

Challenge:

For one week, focus on saving small amounts daily by making smart choices. Try **ONE** of the following methods:

1. The "No-Spend Day" Challenge

- Pick one day this week where you don't spend *any* money.
- Instead, find free alternatives (e.g., bring lunch from home, skip a coffee, do a no-cost activity).
- **Why?** It helps you realize how much you can save by cutting unnecessary expenses.

2. The "Round-Up" Trick

- Every time you spend money, round up your total and save the difference.
- **Example:** If you spend $3.75, put $0.25 into savings.
- **Why?** Small amounts add up quickly without feeling overwhelming.

3. The "Save Before You Spend" Habit

- Before spending *any* money this week, transfer $5–$10 into savings.
- Even if it's just $1 per day, start the habit of saving first, spending second.
- **Why?** You'll train your brain to prioritize saving instead of making it an afterthought.

Reflection:

- Which challenge did you try?
- How much did you save in just one week?

- What was the hardest part?

Part 4: The Habit Challenge – Build One Savings Habit This Week

Choose **ONE** savings habit below and commit to doing it for seven days:

1. The "Invisible Money" Method

- Every time you get money, immediately move 10% to a separate savings account.
- **Why?** If you don't see it, you won't be tempted to spend it.

2. The "$5 Rule"

- Anytime you receive a $5 bill, put it into a savings jar instead of spending it.
- **Why?** This makes saving feel like a game and adds up faster than you think!

3. The "Micro-Saving" Habit

- At the end of each day, put all your loose change (or a small amount like $1) into savings.
- **Why?** Daily habits are easier to maintain than big one-time savings goals.

Reflection:

- Which habit did you choose?

- What was the easiest or hardest part?
- Did this habit change the way you think about saving?

Part 5: Discussion & Group Activity – Saving Smarter

For Educators, Parents, and Homeschoolers

This section will help teens connect the concept of saving to real-life financial situations, making it practical, engaging, and fun. Educators and parents can use these discussion points and activities to encourage critical thinking about saving habits.

Discussion: "Why Do We Struggle to Save?"

Goal: To help teens identify barriers to saving, as well as how to make it easier.

Discussion agenda:

1. Why is saving hard for most people?

- Is it because money feels like it disappears too fast?
- Do impulse buys stop us from saving?
- What emotions do you feel when deciding to save or spend?

2. Think about the last time you had money.

- Did you spend it all or save some?
- If you could go back, would you have made a different choice?

3. What motivates you to save?

- A big future goal (like a car or trip)?

- Just knowing you have money set aside?
- Seeing your savings number grow?

Takeaway: The secret to saving isn't about saying "no"—it's about saying "YES" to something even better in the future!

Activity: "How Long Does It Take to Save?"

Supplies Needed: Calculator, pen, and paper (or a budgeting app)

Instructions

1. Pick a savings goal (e.g., $500 for a trip, $300 for a gadget, $1,000 for a car down payment).
2. Figure out how much you could realistically save per week.
3. Divide your goal by your weekly savings to see how long it would take to reach it.
4. Adjust:
    - What happens if you increase savings by $5 a week?
    - What happens if you cut a small expense and save that instead?
    - Could you reach your goal faster?

Example Calculation

- **Goal:** $300 for new headphones
- **Saving:** $15 per week

- **Time to reach goal:** 20 weeks (5 months)
- *But…* if you save $20 per week instead, **you'd get there in just 15 weeks!**

Discussion

- Did your savings timeline surprise you?
- What's one expense you could cut or reduce to speed up savings?
- Would reaching your goal faster make saving feel more exciting?

Takeaway: Small savings add up *fast* when you stay consistent!

Action Habit 3: Become a Super Saver

The Habit:

Every time you receive money (allowance, gift, paycheck), save a set percentage before spending anything.

Daily Action:

Start small (e.g., 10% of every dollar you get).

Use a savings app or a physical jar to track progress.

Turn saving into a fun challenge (e.g., compete with a friend or set milestones).

Why It Works:

- Helps you save consistently instead of relying on leftovers.
- Builds the habit of paying yourself first.

- Turns saving from a chore into something exciting!

✓ **Challenge:** Try this for seven days and see how much you save. You'll be surprised!

Habit 3 Progress Check: Did You Take Action?

✓ Quick Review

- Did you complete the Self-Assessment on your saving habits?
- Did you try one of the Savings Challenges (No-Spend Day, Round-Up Trick, or Save Before You Spend)?
- Did you set a short-term or long-term savings goal?

✓ Rate Your Progress (1–5 Stars)

★ ★ ★ ★ ★ *(How well did you apply today's lesson?)*

Next Step:

Ready to move on? Nice work! Before moving on, though, take a moment to reflect:

- What's one new thing you learned about saving this week?
- What's your biggest savings goal right now?
- Talk about your thoughts with a teacher, parent, or friend!

After that, get ready to check out the next chapter, where we'll keep this journey to financial know-how going!

Habit 4:

Spending Smarter: Getting What You Want Without Going Broke

It's not about how much you spend, but how you spend it.

Spending smart isn't about pinching every penny or never treating yourself. It's about using your money in a way that gets you the things you truly want *without* leaving you broke, stressed, or filled with regret later. It's not "spend less," it's "spend smarter." *Big* difference.

Let's jump into how you can start mastering this superpower.

Understanding Spending Habits

Needs vs. Wants

Alright, first things first: Not everything you *want* is something you *need.*

A "need" is something you can't live without—food, basic clothes, a way to get to school or work, a place to live.

A "want" is something that's nice to have but you could totally survive without it: the latest AirPods, premium sneakers, extra streaming subscriptions (hint: Netflix isn't a need!).

Quick Check: When you're about to buy something, ask yourself the *Three Easy Peasy Questions*:

1. **Do I need this?** (Will my life fall apart without it?)

2. **Can I afford this?** (Without touching my savings or going into debt?)

3. **Will I regret this?** (In 24 hours, will I wish I had that money back?)

If you answer "no" to 1, "maybe not" to 2, or "probably" to 3... Step away from the checkout.

Real Teen Example: Meet Christopher

Christopher, 17, used to buy random clothes and gadgets every weekend. It felt good—for about five minutes. Then he'd stare at an empty bank account.

Christopher realized something had to change. That's when I shared a simple trick with him: the "3 Questions" test.

Before buying anything, he had to ask himself:

- *Do I need this?*
- *Can I afford this?*
- *Will I regret this later?*

Within a year, Christopher saved over $1,000—enough to buy a used car. Lesson? Small spending decisions equals *huge* life upgrades.

Important Money Fact: What Is Inflation (and Why Should You Care?)

Ever wonder why your favorite snacks, clothes, or even video games seem to cost more every year?

It's not your imagination. It's something called **inflation**—and it's basically the "price rise monster" of the economy.

Easy Peasy Breakdown

- Inflation means that over time, the prices of stuff go up.
- It's not because the things themselves change.
- It's because **the value of money shrinks** a little each year.
- And because each dollar is worth less year after year, you need *more* of your dollars to buy the same stuff you used to get for cheaper.

Example

- 10 years ago, a movie ticket might have cost $7.
- Today, that same ticket could cost $14.

The movie didn't get twice as good—your dollars just don't stretch as far now.

Pro Tip: Even houses don't "*get more valuable*" in a magical way. Mostly, it's the money you buy them with that loses power over time.

This is why saving and smart spending matter. Your money today is worth more than it will be in five years. So, be sure to spend it wisely now!

The Psychology of Spending

Word of advice? Stores are not your friends. They're basically playgrounds designed to separate you from your money.

Here's how they mess with your brain:

1. Store Tricks

- Essentials like milk and bread? Always at the *back* of the supermarket.
- Why? So that you're forced to walk past aisles of candy, snacks, and random gadgets you didn't plan to buy.

2. Sale Madness

- "Limited time offer!"
- "Only 2 left in stock!"
- These phrases make your brain panic: *"What if I miss out?!"*

3. Peer Pressure

- Your friends flex a new phone or designer bag, and suddenly you feel *naked* without it.
- Cue: Unplanned shopping spree.

4. Emotional Spending

- Bad day? Shopping spree.
- Good day? Shopping spree.
- Bored? Yep—shopping spree.

Retail therapy feels good… until the bill shows up.

Easy Peasy Pause Trick: Before you buy something, *pause.* Ask yourself: *Am I buying this because I need it… or because I feel bored, stressed, or* *full of FOMO?* (That stands for "Fear of Missing Out," if you didn't know!)

Social Media Spending Traps

Social media isn't just for memes and TikToks anymore. It's a giant digital mall—and you're walking around with your wallet wide open.

Here's How They Trap You

1. Influencer Pressure:

- That perfect influencer with the "must-have" hoodie?
- Sponsored. Paid. Probably doesn't even like the hoodie.

2. Fake Deals:

- "70% off for the next 2 hours!"
- Translation: Same overpriced stuff that will still be "on sale" tomorrow… and next week.

3. Comparison Game:

- You see everyone living their "best life" online.
- Makes you feel like you're missing out unless you buy the same stuff.

How to Outsmart the Traps

- **Mute temptation:** Unfollow accounts that constantly push products.
- **Reality check:** Remember, their life = curated highlight reel.

- **Build your "Nope" muscle:** Saying "no" to trends today = Saying "yes" to real goals tomorrow.

Quick Reflection: Write down one time you bought something because you saw it online.

- Did you still love it a month later?
- Was it worth the money?

No judgment—just awareness.

Quick Recap

- Learn the difference between needs and wants.
- Watch out for psychological spending traps.
- Recognize when social media tries to hijack your wallet.

Stretching Your Dollars

By now, you're probably thinking,

"Okay Noah, I get it. Saving is cool. But what about when I actually want to spend some of my hard-earned cash?"

Good question, savvy spender. Because here's the deal:

It's not just *how much* you spend—it's *how smart* you spend it that makes all the difference.

With that in mind, let's turn you into a deal-sniffing, money-stretching genius, shall we?

How to Score Deals

Think of this like a treasure hunt.

There are golden deals hidden everywhere—to find them, you just need the right map (and a little patience).

A few tricks of the trade:

- **Use Apps That Hunt Discounts for You:**

Apps like Honey automatically find and apply coupon codes when you shop online. And there are even apps like Rakuten that give you cashback just for clicking through their links. (It's like getting free money for doing what you were gonna do anyway!)

- **Time Your Purchases:**

Did you know clothes are way cheaper *right after* the season ends? Seriously, buying a winter jacket in spring can save you half the price. And honestly, nobody cares if your jacket is "last season"—you'll still be warm, and your wallet will still be happy.

Same goes for tech, furniture, and even games. A little patience equals some major discounts.

- **Wait for the Sale:**

Impulse buying is your wallet's worst enemy. If you can wait just a few weeks (or even days), chances are that that *must-have* item will go on sale.

Easy Peasy Power Move

Make a "Waiting List" in your notes app.

Whenever you want something badly, write it down—and commit to checking back after a month. If you still really want it (and it's cheaper), then it's a double win.

Cash vs. Card

Alright, time for some real talk:

Cards are sneaky.

When you swipe a card, it *feels* like you're not really spending money. But oh, trust me—*you are.*

The Power of Cash:

Spending actual cash *hurts* a little more. (And that's actually a good thing, trust me.) It forces your brain to go, *"Wait... do I really want to part with these bits of green paper?"* Studies even show that people spend up to 20% less when paying with cash instead of a card.

Challenge

Try taking out a set amount of cash for "fun spending" each week—and when it's gone, *it's gone.* No dipping into your card unless it's a true emergency.

- **Managing Your Debit Card Wisely:**

  Debit cards are awesome—if you use them smartly:

  - Set up **low balance alerts** so you don't overspend.
  - Check your banking app weekly to track where your money's going.
  - Stick to *using it for planned purchases only*—not every little craving that pops into your brain.

- **Avoiding Overdrafts and Hidden Fees:**

  Overdraft fees are like sneaky monsters hiding in your bank account. They pounce the second you spend more money than you actually have—and boom! You get charged $30... for being broke.

Easy Peasy Tip

- Always know your balance.
- Turn on automatic blocks (most banks offer them now) so you can't accidentally overspend.

Future You will send you a mental high-five for dodging those expensive traps, for a certainty!

Buying Quality Over Quantity

Ready for some wisdom that sounds boring but saves you *huge* money?

Cheap stuff costs more in the long run.

Example: Cheap Shoes vs. Good Shoes

Let's say you grab a pair of sneakers for $30.

They look decent... for about a month.

But after a few weeks, the sole starts peeling, your feet hurt, and boom—you're shopping for another pair.

Now, fast forward one year:

- You've had to buy around **12 pairs** just to keep up.
- **12 × $30 = $360** burned through sneakers.

Ouch.

And now, compare that to buying a quality $90 pair that lasts two full years.

- Cost per year? **$45**.
- Your feet? Happy.
- Your wallet? Even happier.

Quick Reflection

- Cheap shoes = $360 a year.
- Good shoes = $45 a year.

Again, saving money sometimes means spending smarter, not cheaper.

It goes to show that one good decision upfront saves you *hundreds* down the line. *Easy Peasy*, right?

How to Research Before Buying

When buying anything (clothes, tech, gadgets), be sure to do the following:

- Read **user reviews**—real ones, not the super-fake "five stars no explanation" ones.
- Check **YouTube** for honest unboxing and durability tests.
- Ask friends or family what brands they trust.

Spending a little extra time before you buy saves you *lots* of money later. And remember:

Smart shoppers don't just buy cheaper. They buy *better*.

Quick Recap

What's one thing you regret buying because it broke, wore out, or didn't last? What would you do differently next time?

(Write it down—you'll be amazed how remembering this helps you improve your spending game.)

Staying in Control of Spending

Alright, let's get real. Spending money isn't the enemy. Losing control of your spending? That's what wrecks your wallet—and your future goals.

In this section, we'll sharpen your "money control muscles" so you can spend smarter, not just harder.

Impulse Purchase Triggers

Ever bought something and, like, 10 minutes later thought, "Why did I even *want* this?"

Welcome to the magical world of impulse purchases.

Common Triggers for Impulse Spending

- **Stress:** Shopping feels like a quick dopamine hit.
- **Boredom:** Nothing better to do? Scroll... click... buy.
- **Peer pressure:** Friends are doing it, so... why not?
- **Sales and "Limited Time" offers:** FOMO strikes again.

Easy Peasy Fixes

- **Spot your triggers:** Take note of what situations make you want to spend mindlessly.
- **Find free distractions:** Instead of shopping when you're bored, take a walk, watch a funny YouTube video, practice a hobby, or text a friend.
- **Make a Wish-List, Not a Buy-List:** When you want something, put it on a "wish-list" first. Wait at least a few days. Still want it later? Then maybe it's worth it after all.

Real-Life Teen Scenario

Jason, 16, realized he kept blowing money after late-night TikTok scrolling. Solution? He started keeping a "Late Night Wish List" on his Notes app.

After a week, he realized he didn't actually want half the stuff anymore—and saved over $400 in three months.

Handling Money in Social Situations: Dealing With Peer Pressure & Money Ethics

Money choices aren't just made in front of a screen. They're made in real life—especially around friends.

So, let's tackle **three** of the biggest traps teens face:

1. Resisting Peer Pressure to Overspend

Sometimes it feels like saying "no" = saying "I'm lame."

You get invited to:

- expensive concerts

- fancy restaurants
- shopping trips where you feel pressure to buy "just something" so you don't feel left out

The problem: Spending money you don't have (or don't want to spend) just to fit in.

Smart Response Ideas:

- **"That looks awesome, but it's not in my budget this month."**
- **"I'm saving for something bigger right now."**
- **"Let's find a cheaper option so we can all hang out."**

Real-Life Teen Scenario

Maria, 17, loved her friends but hated how much they spent on Starbucks and mini shopping sprees. So, she started suggesting free park meetups instead—and guess what? Most of her friends were relieved someone finally said it. (Turns out half of them were broke too!)

2. Saying "No" to Financial Favors (Without Feeling Guilty)

We've all had a friend ask, "Hey, can you spot me $20? I'll pay you back next week." Sounds harmless, right? But what if they don't pay you back? Or what if lending the money changes your friendship?

Golden rule: If you can't afford to *give* the money away without resentment, don't lend it.

Polite Script:

- **"I'd love to help, but I'm working on my own savings goals right now."**

- **"I'm not able to lend money, but I can help you figure out other options."**

Real-life teen scenario:

Jamal, 15, once loaned $50 to a friend for a concert ticket.

The friend ghosted him for two months—and the friendship never recovered. Hard lesson, but at least it made Jamal smarter about setting money boundaries early.

3. Recognizing Money Scams & Shady Investments

Quick quiz: Your friend says you can double your money fast if you just join this "opportunity." Should you:

- **(A)** Sign up immediately.
- **(B)** Ask 1,000 skeptical questions.
- **(C)** Run faster than Usain Bolt.

Answer: **(C)**

No question about it. **Run.**

Common Teen Money Scams:

- pyramid schemes ("Recruit your friends and get rich!")
- fake crypto investments
- "guaranteed profit" apps
- sketchy reselling hustles that ask for upfront cash

Quick Money Rule

If it sounds too good to be true? Yup—it's *definitely* too good to be true.

Let's Reflect

- Have you ever felt pressured to spend money you didn't really want to?
- How do you set financial boundaries without feeling weird about it?
- What's the smartest way to help a friend without sacrificing your own goals?

Spending Limits

So, what's one of the easiest ways to stay in control? Well, here's what I recommend: **Set a weekly or monthly spending cap.** Example:

- You could decide that $50 is your fun money for the month.
- Once it's gone, it's gone.
- No cheating. No "just one more coffee" loopholes.

How to Make It Easy

- Use a budgeting app to track your spending live.
- Withdraw the cash you need and leave the cards at home when you go out.
- Celebrate when you stay under budget—like winning a personal championship.

Real-Life Teen Scenario

Ava, 14, set a $10 weekly snack budget. Instead of impulse buying junk every day, she planned her treats ahead—and saved $300 by the end of the school year!

Accountability Partners

Saving and spending smarter gets way easier when you're not flying solo.

How to Use Accountability

- Pick a friend, parent, or mentor you trust.
- Tell them your spending goal (e.g., "I'm cutting snack spending by half this month.")
- Check in once a week.
- Celebrate wins—yes, even the tiny ones.

Fun Idea

Create a spending smarter challenge with your friends:

- Set a weekly spending limit (e.g., $20 for snacks or entertainment).
- Share your smartest purchase each week—who got the most value for the least cash?
- Most creative or cost-effective "win" gets bragging rights (or a free coffee from the group).

Most teens think smart spending means sacrificing fun—but turn it into a challenge, and suddenly you're not missing out… you're taking control and winning at life.

Habit 4: Key Chapter Takeaway: Spending Smarter = Buying Freedom

I've said it before, I'll say it again: Spending money isn't bad. But spending money without thinking? *That's* what messes people up.

This chapter wasn't about making you feel guilty for buying things.

It was about learning how to **spend with purpose**—so *you* stay in charge, not your *impulses*. Throughout this chapter, you learned how to:

- tell the difference between real needs and tempting wants.
- stretch your dollars without stretching your stress levels—finding deals, using cash wisely, and picking quality over junk.
- stay strong when impulse buying, peer pressure, or money scams try to mess with your vibe.

But there's one more secret to master: Spending smarter isn't just a one-time thing. It's a **habit** you build, one decision at a time. And you already know the winning CRR formula, don't you?

Cue → Routine → Reward

On that note, here's how I want you to apply it when it comes to spending:

- **Cue:** You're about to spend money (you spot something cool, friends invite you out, your favorite brand drops a new garment).
- **Routine:** Pause. Ask yourself the ***Three Easy Peasy Spending Questions***:

1. **Do I need this?** (Will my life fall apart without it?)
2. **Can I afford this?** (Without touching my savings or going into debt?)
3. **Will I regret this?** (In 24 hours, will I wish I had that money back?)

Reward: You either make a purchase you truly value *or* you keep your cash and move closer to a bigger goal.

Every time you run this loop, your brain gets stronger at **choosing freedom over FOMO.**

At first, it takes a little effort. Later, though, it becomes second nature.

Soon enough, you'll barely even think about it—you'll just be *that* person who spends like a total boss.

Interactive Challenges:

Take Control of Your Spending

Part 1: Self-Assessment – What Type of Spender Are You?

Choose the statement that best describes you:

- **(A)** "I spend money as soon as I get it and don't really think about it."
- **(B)** "I try to be careful with my spending, but I sometimes buy things on impulse."

- **(C)** "I plan most of my spending, but sometimes I make exceptions."
- **(D)** "I carefully track and plan my spending to stay in control."

Reflection: If you chose A or B, look back over this chapter—it's here to help you take charge of your spending habits, after all. If you chose C or D, you're already on the right path—let's level up your skills!

Part 2: Real-Life Scenario – What Would You Do?

Scenario 4

You're at the mall with friends, and you spot a **limited edition pair of jeans** on sale for **$120**. You **weren't planning** to buy anything today, but you have **$150** in your account. Your friends encourage you to buy them, saying they might sell out fast.

Choose one:

- **(A)** Buy the jeans immediately—opportunities like this don't come often!
- **(B)** Walk away and think about it for 24 hours—if you still want them, come back.
- **(C)** Only buy them if you can cut back on another expense this month.
- **(D)** Look for a better deal online or see if you can buy them second-hand.

Reflection: What choice helps you balance **enjoying your money versus managing it wisely**? How would a financially smart person approach this?

Part 3: Smart Spending Challenge – Cut Unnecessary Costs for One Week

Challenge:

For the next seven days, find some creative ways to reduce your spending while still enjoying life. Try **ONE** of the following:

1. The "Spending Fast" Challenge

- Pick a category (e.g., snacks, clothes, online shopping) and **spend $0 on it for a week**.
- **Why?** Helps you break spending habits and see what you can live without.

2. The "Swap & Save" Challenge

- Instead of **buying something new**, swap, borrow, or find a free alternative.
- **Example:** Borrow a book instead of buying, do a clothing swap with friends.
- **Why?** This builds smart money habits and saves cash without missing out.

3. The "Cash-Only" Experiment

- Withdraw a set amount of cash for **fun spending** and **use only that** for the week.
- **Why?** Help's you feel the impact of spending and stick to a budget.

Reflection:

- Which challenge did you pick?
- What was the hardest part?
- Did this help you think differently about your spending?

Part 4: The Habit Challenge – Build One Smart Spending Habit This Week

Choose **ONE** spending habit below and commit to doing it for seven days:

1. The "Wait 48 Hours" Rule

- Before buying anything over **$50, wait 48 hours** before making a decision.
- **Why?** It helps you avoid impulse buys and decide if it's truly worth it.

2. The "Price vs. Value" Test

- Before making a purchase, ask: **"Will this last me at least six months?"**
- If yes, consider buying. If not, reconsider.
- **Why?** It helps shift focus from **cheap & trendy** to **long-lasting value**.

3. The "Cost Per Use" Formula

- Before buying something expensive, calculate:

Price ÷ Number of Times You'll Use It = Cost Per Use

- **Example:** A $200 jacket worn **100 times** = **$2 per wear** (good value!).
- **Why?** It helps you spend **smarter**, not just **cheaper**.

Reflection:

- Which habit did you choose?
- What surprised you about your spending patterns?
- Did it change the way you think about **wants vs. needs**?

Part 5: Discussion & Group Activity – Smarter Spending

For Educators, Parents, and Homeschoolers

This section is designed to help teens think critically about their spending habits, recognize impulse buying triggers, and develop practical strategies to make smarter purchasing decisions. Educators and parents can use these engaging discussions and hands-on activities to bring spending lessons to life!

Discussion: "Would You Buy That Again?"

Goal: Help teens reflect on their past spending decisions and recognize patterns.

Discussion agenda:

1. **Think about a purchase you made in the last 3 months.**
   - What did you buy, and why?
   - Did you love it and use it often, or forget about it after a week?

- If you could go back, would you buy it again?

2. Impulse vs. intentional spending

- Have you ever bought something just because your friends had it?
- What's the difference between wanting something in the moment vs. wanting it long-term?
- How can waiting 24-48 hours help make better decisions?

3. How much do small expenses add up?

- If you spend $5 on snacks every day, how much is that per week? Per year?
- If you cut back just once a week, what could you save in a year?
- How could you redirect that money toward a goal that matters more?

Takeaway: Every dollar you spend is a choice. Would you rather have this item, or would you rather reach a bigger goal?

Activity: "The True Cost of a Purchase"

Supplies Needed: Pen, paper, calculator (or budgeting app)

Instructions:

1. Pick an item you really want (e.g., some new shoes, a gaming console).
2. Write down how much it costs.
3. Calculate how many hours of work or chores it would take to afford it.

Example: If the new shoes cost $120 and you earn $10 per hour, that's 12 hours of work!

4. Now, answer these questions:

- Is the item worth that much of your time?
- Would you still buy it if you had to earn the money first?
- What else could you do with that money instead?

Discussion

- Does thinking about spending in hours worked change how valuable an item feels?
- Would you be more careful with impulse spending if you had to work extra hours to afford it?
- What's one strategy you can use this week to spend smarter?

Takeaway: When you spend money, you're also spending time. Make sure it's worth it!

Action Habit 4: Become a Mindful Spender

The Habit:

Before making a purchase, ask yourself these **3 questions:**

1. **Is this a need or a want?**
2. **Will I still value this in a month?**
3. **Is there a smarter way to buy this (cheaper, second-hand, or on sale)?**

Daily Action:

- Pause before impulse-buying and go through the 3-question test.
- Start tracking **how many times you say NO to unnecessary purchases**—make it a game!
- Find **one area** where you can **cut back** and **redirect that money** to a savings goal.

Why It Works:

- Builds **self-control** over spending habits.
- Helps you focus on **quality over quantity**.
- Reduces **buyer's remorse** and saves money for things that truly matter.

✓ **Challenge:** Try this for **seven days** and track how your spending changes!

Habit 4 Progress Check: Did You Take Action?

✓ Quick Review

- Did you complete the Self-Assessment on your spending habits?
- Did you try one of the Smart Spending Challenges (Spending Fast, Swap & Save, or Cash-Only Experiment)?
- Did you track at least **one** impulse spending decision and pause before making the purchase?

✓ **Rate Your Progress (1–5 Stars)**

★★★★★ *(How well did you apply today's lesson?)*

Next Step

Ready to move on? Great work! Before moving on, take a moment to reflect:

- What's one thing you learned about spending this week?
- Have you ever regretted a purchase? What did you learn from it?
- Talk about your thoughts with a teacher, parent, or friend!

Then, when you're ready, we'll dive into the next chapter and keep levelling up your financial skills!

Habit 5:

Earning More – Side Hustles and Small Business Ideas

What if you could earn $500 in your free time? Here's how to make it happen.

Most people think you need to be an adult with a full-time job to start making real money. Not true. If you're willing to get a little creative, put in some effort, and learn a few basic skills, you can start stacking cash right now—even before you graduate.

Let's dive into some smart ways you can start earning money that fits around your school life, your hobbies, and your future goals.

Finding Side Hustles That Fit

Building your own income stream starts by picking the right side hustle—something you enjoy (or at least don't hate), that pays fairly, and that you can actually stick with.

Here are three major ways to find your fit:

Part-Time Jobs

When you're just starting out, nothing beats the good old-fashioned part-time job. Babysitting, tutoring, dog walking, lawn mowing, or helping neighbors with odd jobs—these gigs are easy ways to start earning because they don't require any fancy qualifications.

And when you're starting out, consistency matters more than pay. A steady $20 here, $30 there, adds up fast when you build a habit of working.

Real-Life Teen Scenario

Olivia, 16, started babysitting on weekends for a family friend. It wasn't glamorous work, but by sticking with it and building a solid reputation, she made over $1,000 in just a few months.

Later, she used that money to upgrade her laptop and invest in starting her own small tutoring business online.

Key Takeaway: You don't need a "dream job" to start earning—you just need that first job.

Pro Tip: Babysitting and dog walking often grow through word of mouth. Always ask your happy customers if they know anyone else who needs help!

Online Gigs

If leaving the house sounds like too much work, good news: you can also earn money online.

Thanks to the internet, there are more opportunities than ever for teens to freelance and build skills while earning money.

Here are some ideas:

- **Selling Crafts on Etsy**: If you're good at making jewelry, stickers, digital art, or anything handmade, Etsy is a ready-made marketplace.

- **Freelancing on Fiverr**: Fiverr lets you offer services like graphic design, writing, editing TikToks, or even making memes.

- **Microtasks on Apps**: Apps like TaskRabbit allow teens in some areas to pick up small jobs like running errands or assembling furniture.

Real-Life Teen Scenario

Diego, 17, had a talent for graphic design. He started offering simple $10 TikTok banner designs on Fiverr. And within a few months, he was earning about $500 a month, all by working only a few hours a week after school.

Key Tip: You don't need to be a professional. Many people just want some affordable help. So, if you're a little better than average at something, you're already valuable to someone.

Important Note: Always check age requirements and get a parent's permission before signing up for platforms.

Leveraging Your Talents

Your hobbies aren't just for fun—they can also be gold mines for earning money. Seriously, think about what you're already good at:

- Play guitar? Offer some beginner lessons.
- Love photography? Offer cheap photo sessions for birthdays or events.
- Good at baking? Sell custom cupcakes for parties.

Turning hobbies into cash is often the most fun way to earn because you get paid for doing something you already enjoy!

Real-Life Teen Scenario

Maya, 15, loved baking cookies. So, she started selling small cookie boxes to neighbors and family friends for $10 each. In one holiday season alone, she made over $700—enough to fund a trip she had been dreaming about!

Spotting Market Gaps

Another great trick is spotting gaps around you. Maybe your neighborhood is full of busy parents who need after-school babysitters. Or small businesses nearby who need someone to update their Instagram pages. The point is, opportunities are everywhere—you just need to look.

Marketing Yourself

If you want to get really serious, try building a simple Instagram page that showcases your work. Post a few examples, ask satisfied customers for quick testimonials, and start telling friends and family what you offer. When you make it easy for people to find you, word spreads faster than you think!

Let's Reflect

Think about two or three things you're already good at or enjoy doing. Could any of these become your first side hustle?

Starting a Small Business

Now, if you're serious about leveling up your money game, then at some point, you're going to realize this simple truth: jobs are great... but businesses give you control. When you work a job, you trade time for money. When you start a small business, you build something that can keep growing—sometimes even while you sleep.

And the best time to start experimenting with this? Right now.

You have a major advantage: low risk, high opportunity.

Let's break it down.

Why Teens Make Great Entrepreneurs

First off, let's kill the myth that you have to wait until you're "older" to start a business. In fact, teens often make *better* entrepreneurs than adults. Here's why:

- **Low-risk environment**: Most teens don't have to worry about paying rent, feeding a family, or covering utility bills. That means you can afford to take risks, learn from mistakes, and try different ideas without your whole world crashing down.

- **Time to learn**: You've got school and homework, sure—but you still have pockets of free time that adults would kill for.

- **Natural creativity**: Teens are often way better at spotting trends, understanding what's cool, and adapting quickly.

Real Teen Success Stories

- **Lemonade Stands**: I know, sounds basic, but it's such a classic! And besides, plenty of kids have flipped a basic lemonade stand into a full summer income!

- **Handmade Crafts**: Seriously, teens making custom bracelets, candles, and stickers are cleaning up on Etsy and Instagram.

- **Online Boutiques**: Some teens build simple Instagram shops selling thrifted clothes, custom shoes, or vintage finds—and make hundreds or even thousands per month!

Key Takeaway: You don't need a million-dollar idea. You just need *a small idea you're willing to actually start.*

Step-By-Step Guide to Starting

So, how do you actually start your own small hustle? Well, it's way less complicated than you might think. Here's the no-fluff, *Easy Peasy Guide*:

Step 1: Pick an Idea

Start simple.

Look around your skills, your hobbies, and your community. Here are some examples:

- tutoring younger kids in a subject you're good at
- selling handmade crafts like jewelry, candles, or art
- flipping thrifted clothes or vintage finds online
- running errands for busy neighbors

In short, if it solves a problem or adds value, it's a real business.

Step 2: Set a Small Budget and Track Profits

Before spending anything, ask yourself:

- What do I need to get started? (Supplies, basic materials, maybe a Canva subscription if you're designing?)
- How much will it cost upfront?
- How much will I charge?

Always track every dollar you spend and every dollar you make. Even a simple notebook or a free app like Google Sheets works. Why? Because tracking turns your "cute little hustle" into a real business mindset. You'll learn what's profitable—and what's not—way faster.

Step 3: Build a Simple Website or Social Media Page

You don't need to hire a fancy web designer.

- Use free tools like Canva to create clean Instagram posts.
- Start a free business page on Instagram or TikTok showing what you offer.
- And if you want to go extra pro, use free sites like Linktree to collect your links in one place.

The key? Make it easy for people to find you, see what you offer, and contact you. Remember: *People buy from people they trust.*

Show up consistently, be clear about what you offer, and be professional—even if your "office" is your bedroom.

Dealing With Challenges

Let's be honest—starting a business sounds exciting, but real life brings real challenges. The good news? Every challenge is actually an opportunity to build skills most adults *still* struggle with.

Here's how to tackle the big ones:

Time Management: How to Balance School and Work

- **Set clear work hours:** Maybe you work on your hustle only after homework or just weekends.
- **Use a simple planner or phone calendar:** Block off time so you're not winging it.
- **Prioritize school:** Missing grades for quick money isn't a smart trade-off.

Remember: Hustles should fit *around* your education—not destroy it.

Staying Motivated When Business Is Slow

News flash: It won't always be busy.

There will be slow days. There will be boring days. There will be "Why am I even doing this?" days. But here's the thing: that's *normal.* Real entrepreneurs don't quit at the first slow patch. They adapt, they learn, they improve.

Pro Tip:

- Use slow days to level up your skills, redesign your marketing, or brainstorm new offers.
- Sometimes slow seasons are exactly when you make your biggest leaps.

Learning From Mistakes: Why Failure Is Part of Success

Maybe your first idea flops. Maybe you undercharge. Maybe you mess up an order. Guess what, though? These scenarios all warrant some congratulations. Why? Because you're officially a real entrepreneur now.

Look, every mistake teaches you something that success never could. The faster you make small mistakes, the faster you get better.

Easy Peasy Rule: Mistakes = Feedback. Feedback = Growth.

Growth = *Future wins.*

Let's Reflect

- What's one small hustle you could start today with $20 or less?

- If it failed, what would you learn that would make your next hustle stronger?

Growing Your Earnings

Alright, you've got the skills. You've got the side hustle ideas. Now it's time to level up.

Growing your earnings isn't just about doing more work—it's about working smarter, building momentum, and setting yourself up for serious wins in the future.

Let's break down exactly how to stretch your income muscles—the *Easy Peasy* way.

Active Income vs. Passive Income: What's the Difference?

Before we get into hustling harder, let's pause for a second and talk about something major: the two types of income.

Active Income

- This is money you earn by directly working.
- This means you're trading your time and energy for cash.
- Examples include babysitting, tutoring, mowing lawns, designing TikTok banners, and so on.

Passive Income

- This is money that keeps flowing even when you're *not* actively working every second.

- You do the work once, and then it keeps paying you.
- Some examples here are selling an ebook you wrote, getting ad revenue from a YouTube video, or renting out a camera you own.

Pros and Cons

- Active income = faster cash now, but it requires your constant effort.
- Passive income = slower to build, but it eventually earns you cash while you sleep.

Easy Peasy Tip: Start by stacking active income (side hustles, part-time work), then invest some of that money into building passive income streams.

(And yes—in later chapters, we'll dive into investing and even how to build financial freedom, where your *passive income covers your living expenses*! So, definitely stay tuned for Chapters 6 and 8—they're serious game-changers.)

Alright, back to building your earnings…

Passive Income Ideas for Teens

Once you've got some money flowing in, it's time to think smarter about how to keep it growing.

Here, then, are some beginner-friendly passive income ideas you can actually start as a teen:

Rent Out Stuff You Own

Got a bike, camera, or some sports equipment? You could rent this stuff out to neighbors, classmates, or local Facebook groups.

Example: Liam, 15, made $300 in one summer by renting out his GoPro to friends going on vacations.

Create Digital Products

Make an ebook, Canva templates, or a few simple digital art packs. Sell them on Etsy, Gumroad, or other platforms.

Example: Sarah, 16, made $500 selling printable planners for students.

YouTube and Blogging

Start a YouTube channel or blog about something you love. Over time, as you gain viewers, you can earn from ads, sponsorships, or merchandise.

Example: Peter, 17, made $1,200 in a year from his YouTube channel reviewing budget tech gadgets.

Remember: Passive income doesn't mean "zero effort"—it just means "do the work once, and get paid multiple times."

Easy Peasy Mindset Shift: Think about how every side hustle could eventually become passive. Can you teach what you do? Can you turn a service into a product?

Networking and Mentorship

You don't have to figure everything out alone. In fact, the smartest earners *always* get advice and feedback from others.

Here's how you can build your money "dream team":

Find Adults Who Can Help

- Teachers, coaches, neighbors, family members—you'd be surprised who's willing to share advice if you just ask.
- A pro tip here? Ask about their first jobs or businesses—people *love* sharing their stories, trust me.

Join Teen Entrepreneur Groups

- Look for local clubs, online groups, or even virtual summits for young entrepreneurs.
- These communities can connect you with opportunities and inspire you with real teen success stories.

Shadow Small Business Owners

- Ask local shop owners if you can volunteer or shadow them for a few days.
- You'll learn *way* more about real-world business skills than from any TikTok video.

See, networking isn't about being pushy or fake. It's about being curious, asking good questions, and learning from people who've already walked the path you want to take.

Let's Reflect

- Who in your life could teach you something about earning?
- Who do you admire for how they handle money or business? Write down 2–3 names. Then, think about how you could reach out (If this is Mom or Dad, hopefully it's not too much of a thinker!).

Scaling Your Hustle

Once your hustle is rolling, don't just sit back. **Scale it.**

Here's how:

Reinvest Your Profits

- Use some of the money you earn to upgrade your tools.
- **Example:** If you're a freelance video editor, invest in better software. Better quality = higher prices.

Offer New Services to Existing Customers

- Babysitting for a family? Offer pet-sitting too.
- Tutoring a student? Offer to tutor their siblings.
- Already selling handmade crafts? Add custom orders!

Collaborate With Friends

- Team up with a friend who's good at something you're not.
- **Example:** If you're good at baking and your friend's great at graphic design, why not team up to sell cookies with some killer packaging?

Scaling isn't about working twice as hard—it's about working *twice as smart.*

Easy Peasy Bonus Tip: Every time you improve, ask yourself: "Is there a way to make this easier, faster, or bigger without burning out?"

That's how side hustles grow into serious income streams over time.

Habit 5: Key Chapter Takeaway

Earning Money = Earning Freedom

This chapter wasn't just about hustling for a few extra bucks. It was about *learning a skill that changes your entire future.*

When you know how to make your own money—no matter your age, background, or starting point—you unlock a kind of freedom most people spend their whole lives chasing.

In this chapter, you learned how to:

- find a side hustle that fits your skills, time, and interests.
- start your own small business (even with just $20 and a notebook).
- understand the difference between active and passive income—and how to use both to build serious wealth.
- grow your hustle by learning, networking, reinvesting, and thinking bigger.

But here's the real secret:

Making money isn't a one-time thing. It's a habit.

Just like spending smarter, you have to train your brain to spot opportunities, take action, and stick with it—even when it's slow or uncomfortable at first.

And you already know the winning CRR formula:

Cue → Routine → Reward

Here's how it works when it comes to building your earning habit:

- **Cue:** You spot an opportunity to earn (a neighbor needs a dog walker, a classmate needs math help, a friend wants a birthday cake).
- **Routine:** You take action. Offer your services, ask for the job, start small but professional.
- **Reward:** You earn money, gain confidence, and open new doors for bigger opportunities.

Every time you complete this loop, you strengthen your "*Income Muscle.*"

It starts small—but the more you flex it, the stronger it gets.

Big Truth

Your first $20 earned from a side hustle might seem tiny today, but it's the same exact skill you'll use later to earn your first $1,000... your first *$10,000*... and beyond!

Earning money isn't magic. It's momentum.

The earlier you start building that momentum, the sooner you'll hit bigger milestones—like investing (Habit 6) and financial freedom (Habit 8), where your money eventually works harder than you do.

You're not just earning cash. You're earning control over your future. And that's priceless.

Interactive Challenges:

Take Control of Your Earnings

Part 1: Self-Assessment – What's Your Earning Mindset?

Choose the statement that best describes you:

- **(A)** "I've never thought about earning my own money before."
- **(B)** "I'd love to earn extra money, but I don't know where to start."
- **(C)** "I've tried side hustles before but haven't made much money."
- **(D)** "I have a side hustle or part-time job and I'm looking to grow my income."

Reflection: If you chose A or B, never fear—this chapter has your back. Feel free to take another look—you'll be earning money in no time. Meanwhile, if you chose C or D, nice effort—but why not take some of this chapter's tips to heart and start scaling your earnings?

Part 2: Real-Life Scenario – What Would You Do?

Scenario 5

You want to start earning your own money, and you have **two options**:

1. A **part-time job at a coffee shop** paying **$12/hour**, but with strict hours and little flexibility.

2. A **freelance gig tutoring kids** in math for **$15/hour**, but you have to find your own students.

Choose one:

- **(A)** Take the coffee shop job—it's a guaranteed paycheck.
- **(B)** Start tutoring—it pays more, and you control your schedule.
- **(C)** Try both for a few weeks and see which one works better.
- **(D)** Look for a third option that combines flexibility and good pay.

Reflection: What factors matter most to you when choosing how to earn your money—**stability, flexibility, or income potential**?

Part 3: Earning Challenge – Test Your Side Hustle for One Week

Challenge:

Try **one** of the following small income-earning activities for **seven days** to test your earning potential.

1. The "$20 Challenge"

- Find a way to **earn at least $20 this week** using a side hustle idea.
- Babysitting, tutoring, selling old clothes, flipping items—**be creative!**
- **Why?** Helps you see that making money **doesn't have to be hard or complicated**.

2. The "Hobby to Hustle" Test

- Pick something you're already good at (drawing, baking, editing videos) and see if you can make money from it.
- **Example:** Sell **one** drawing, offer to bake cookies for a neighbor, or help a friend with a project for a small fee.
- **Why?** Helps you turn **skills into income**.

3. The "Flip & Profit" Challenge

- Find **one** item you don't use anymore (clothes, gadgets, books).
- Sell it online (Facebook Marketplace, eBay, Depop, etc.).
- **Why?** Learning to **sell things for profit** is a valuable skill!

Reflection:

- Which challenge did you choose?
- How much money did you make?
- Did this change how you view **earning potential?**

Part 4: The Habit Challenge – Build One Earning Habit This Week

Choose ONE earning habit below and commit to doing it for seven days:

1. The "Skill Upgrade" Habit

- Spend **10–15 minutes a day** improving a skill that can help you make money (e.g., graphic design, writing, coding).

- **Why?** The more valuable your skills, the more you can earn!

2. The "Ask for Opportunities" Habit

- Tell **three people** (teachers, friends, neighbors) that you're available for work (tutoring, lawn care, babysitting, etc.).
- **Why?** You never know where **opportunities might come from**!

3. The "$5 a Day" Habit

- Find a way to **earn at least $5 every day for a week.**
- **Why?** Even small amounts **add up quickly** when done consistently.

Reflection:

- Which habit did you choose?
- What surprised you about making money?
- How can you **keep growing your earnings** over time?

Part 5: Discussion & Group Activity – Earning Money & Side Hustles

For Educators, Parents, and Homeschoolers

This section is designed to get teens thinking about their earning potential, identifying opportunities, and developing a proactive mindset about money. Through engaging discussions and hands-on activities, they'll explore how they can earn, grow, and manage their income wisely.

Discussion: "How Would You Make $100 This Month?"

Goal: Encourage teens to brainstorm creative ways to earn money based on their skills, resources, and interests.

Discussion agenda:

1. Think about a time you earned money (or helped someone with a task that could have been paid).

- What was the job, and how did you get it?
- Did you enjoy it? Would you do it again?
- What skills did you use?

2. If you had to make $100 in one month, how would you do it?

- What skills do you already have that people would pay for?
- Could you sell something you no longer use?
- What's one easy side hustle you could start this week?

3. Time vs. Effort: Working Smarter, Not Harder

- Would you rather work 10 hours at a job or spend five hours selling a product or service?
- What's the difference between earning actively (hourly work) and passively (selling something you already made)?
- How can you increase what you earn without working longer hours?

Takeaway: Money is everywhere—you just need to know how to spot opportunities!

Activity: "What's in Your House?" – Finding Hidden Income

Supplies Needed: A pen and some paper, or a notes app on your phone

Instructions:

1. Find three things you don't use or need anymore.

- Clothes, books, gadgets, toys, school supplies—anything still in good condition!

2. Estimate how much each item could sell for.

- Check online prices (eBay, Facebook Marketplace, Depop).

3. Plan how you'd sell them.

- Would you list them online? Sell to friends or family?

4. Extra challenge:

- Pitch your sale to the group—convince someone why they should buy your item!

Discussion

- Were you surprised by how much money you had sitting in your house?
- What other creative ways could you make money without getting a job?
- If you had to flip or improve something to sell for more, what would it be?

Takeaway: There's money hidden everywhere! Learning to sell things is a skill that can help you earn at any age.

Action Habit 5: Become an Income Builder

The Habit:

Set **one small income goal** for the next month—**and make it happen!**

Daily Action:

- Decide how much you want to earn ($50, $100, $200+).
- Choose a method (job, side hustle, flipping items, freelancing).
- Track your progress—celebrate small wins!

Why It Works:

- Helps you **see money-making as a skill** you can improve.
- Builds **confidence**—you'll never feel stuck financially.
- Shows you that **small income streams add up** over time.

✓ **Challenge:** Set a **realistic income goal** and **track how much you make** in one month!

Habit 5 Progress Check: Did You Take Action?

✓ Quick Review

- Did you complete the Self-Assessment on your earning mindset?

- Did you try one of the earning challenges ($20 Challenge, Hobby to Hustle, or Flip & Profit)?
- Did you commit to one earning habit for seven days, such as improving a money-making skill, asking for work opportunities, or earning at least $5 a day?

✓ Rate Your Progress (1–5 Stars)

★ ★ ★ ★ ★ ***(How well did you apply today's lesson?)***

Next Step

Ready to move on? Great job! Before moving on, take a moment to reflect:

- What's one skill or side hustle you could start today?
- What's something you learned about making money?
- Talk about your ideas with a teacher, parent, or friend!

With that all said and done, let's flip to the next chapter and keep building your income skills!

Habit 6:

The Beginner's Guide to Investing

The earlier you start investing, the easier it is to become a millionaire. Don't wait—time is your greatest weapon.

Why Investing Matters

From Hustling for Money to Making Money Hustle for You

In the last chapter, you learned how to hustle, save, and start stacking your first dollars through side gigs and small businesses. That's what we call **active income**—money you earn by trading your time and skills.

But here's the next level: What if you could make your money work for you—even while you're sleeping, studying, or hanging out with friends?

That's the power of **investing**. In fact, investing is one of the best examples of **passive income**—money you keep earning without having to clock in hours every day.

So, from learning how to trade your time for money in Habit 5 (active income), you're now learning how to take some of that earned money and set it up to keep growing by itself (passive income). That's the real magic of passive income — and investing is how most people eventually build wealth without working forever.

It's the secret move that separates people who just make money... from people who build lasting wealth, and the earlier you start, the bigger your advantage.

As Warren Buffett once famously said, **"If you don't find a way to make money while you sleep, you will work until you die."** (Look him up sometime, he's like the Tom Brady of investing.)

What Is Investing?

Investing simply means using your money to buy things—like stocks, bonds, or even businesses that you believe will grow in value over time.

So, instead of leaving your money sitting in a piggy bank or savings account doing nothing, investing **puts it to work.**

Just like with saving, you can think of investing a lot like planting a tree. You plant the seed today, water it over time, and eventually it grows into something strong, powerful, and valuable.

But okay, why not just save money instead, then?

Good question. Here's why:

Saving is important—but saving alone isn't enough.

Remember inflation? That thing that raises the cost of things over time? Well, for this reason, your money slowly loses buying power if it just sits around.

Example:

- Today, $100 might buy you 20 trips to your favorite burger joint.
- In 10 years, that same $100 might only buy you 12 trips.

So sure, saving is safe—but investing is how you stay **ahead of inflation** and grow your wealth faster than prices rise.

Real-Life Example

Imagine you saved $1,000 under your mattress today. Ten years later, you still have $1,000—but it buys you less stuff because prices went up.

Now, imagine you invested that $1,000 and earned an average return of 7% a year (which is historically normal for the stock market). After 10 years, your $1,000 would have grown to nearly **$2,000**—without you working any extra hours!

That's the magic of letting your money hustle for you.

The Power of Compound Interest

Alright, now for the real superpower behind investing: **compound interest**. It might sound complicated at first, but it's actually mind-blowingly simple.

Compound interest just means **earning interest on your interest**. At first, it seems slow. But over time, it snowballs into something massive.

Here's a simple way to see it:

- Let's say you invest $100.
- After a year, you earn $5 in interest (5% return), so now you have $105.
- Next year, you earn 5% interest again—not just on the $100 you put in, but on the $105 you now have.
- And so on, year after year...

Each year, your money grows into a slightly bigger pile. It's like stacking one win on top of another, really!

Visual Example

Let's say you invest just **$170 every month** starting at age 16.

If you keep doing it consistently—and your investments grow by 7% per year—then by the time you turn 40, you would have around **$120,000**.

And that's not by investing thousands at once, mind you—that's just by way of a small, steady commitment every month. As Albert Einstein famously said, "Compound interest is the eighth wonder of the world. He who understands it, earns it. He who doesn't, pays it."

To point out the obvious, you definitely want to be in the first group—the ones who *understand and earn it.*

Starting Small, Dreaming Big

A lot of teens (and even adults) think they need thousands of dollars to start investing. Guess what? Not true at all. Apps like **Robinhood**, **Acorns**, **Greenlight**, and **Fidelity Youth** make it possible to start investing with as little as $5–$10. So, no—you don't need to be rich. You just need to be consistent. Consistency beats big, one-time efforts every single time.

Real-Life Teen Scenario

Marcus, 17, decided to invest $20 a month from his dog-walking money instead of spending it all.

By the time he turned 21, he had built up more than $1,300—just by investing tiny amounts and letting compound interest do its thing.

Quick Recap

- Saving is good, but investing helps your money grow faster than inflation.

- Compound interest is your new best friend—small, consistent investments snowball into something huge over time.
- You don't need a lot of money to start—you just need to start.
- The earlier you begin investing, the easier it is to build real wealth and freedom.

How to Start Investing

Alright, you get the big idea: investing equals growing your money while you focus on life.

Now, let's roll up our sleeves and actually figure out *how* to get started—in a way that's smart, safe, and simple.

Important Disclaimer: Read This Before You Start

All investing carries risk. You can lose money. Always do your research or speak to a trusted adult before investing.

Understanding Investment Options

First, you need to know where your money can go in order to genuinely start growing. So, here's a beginner's guide to the most important types of investments:

Stocks: Owning Tiny Pieces of Companies

A **stock** is simply a tiny piece of ownership in a company. When you buy a share of a stock, you literally own a small slice of that business.

Stocks usually come in two flavors:

- **Growth Stocks:** These are companies focused on growing fast. They often don't pay you cash (called dividends) because they're reinvesting their profits to grow bigger. Example: Companies like Tesla or Amazon.
- **Dividend Stocks:** These are companies that pay you part of their profits regularly, kind of like getting a paycheck just for owning their stock. Example: Companies like Coca-Cola or Johnson & Johnson.

Easy Peasy Tip

- Growth stocks can soar high but also bounce around wildly.
- Dividend stocks grow slower, but they pay you a little income along the way.

So, which one's better? Depends on your goals. (And spoiler alert: owning a mix is usually the smartest move!)

Index Funds vs. Individual Stocks

Imagine trying to pick a winning stock... It's like guessing which player will score the most points in a basketball game.

Now, imagine betting on the whole team instead of just one player. That's what an **index fund** does.

An index fund is a collection of many stocks bundled together, often tracking a whole market like the S&P 500 (which includes 500 of the biggest companies in America).

Key differences:

- **Individual Stocks** = Riskier, but can grow faster if you choose well.

- **Index Funds** = Safer, slower, more stable way to grow your money steadily.

Easy Peasy Rule: If you don't want to spend hours researching companies, stick to index funds. It's like putting your money into a winning team instead of betting on a single player.

Bonds: The Safe, Boring Cousins

Bonds are loans that you give to governments or companies. They promise to pay you back later with a little extra as interest.

Bonds are usually safer than stocks, but they grow your money more slowly.

Simple way to think about it:

- Stocks = Fast cars (higher speed, higher risk)
- Bonds = Bicycles (slower, but steady and reliable)

Most smart investors eventually own a mix of stocks *and* bonds to balance growth and safety.

Investing Apps and Tools for Teens

You don't need a Wall Street broker or a million-dollar account to start investing. In fact, you can literally start from your phone today.

Here are some beginner-friendly options:

Best Investing Apps for Teens

- **Stash:** Lets you start investing with just $5. Helps you learn with mini-lessons built into the app.

- **Fidelity Youth:** One of the few legit teen investing accounts, made specifically for ages 13–17 (with parent supervision).

- **Greenlight:** Started as a debit card app, now includes investing features. Great if you want to learn budgeting and investing together.

Setting Up a Custodial Account

Since you're still under 18, you'll need a **custodial account—**a fancy way of saying an adult (like your parent or guardian) helps manage the account until you're legally an adult.

How it works:

- You and your parent open the account together.

- You control the decisions (what to invest in), but your parent legally oversees it until you're 18 or 21 (depending on your state).

Pro Tip: Treat it like your own mini business. Research your choices. Take it seriously. The earlier you start acting like a real investor, the faster your money will grow.

Robo-Advisors: Investing Made Brain-Dead Easy

If picking stocks sounds stressful, don't worry. **Robo-advisors** are apps that invest your money automatically based on your goals and risk tolerance.

Some popular beginner robo-advisors:

- **Acorns:** Rounds up your purchases and invests your spare change.

- **Betterment:** Sets up smart portfolios with zero stress.

Think of it like putting your money on autopilot, so it grows while you focus on school, sports, and chilling with friends.

Avoiding Common Mistakes

Before you run off to open an account, let's pump the brakes for a second. Here are a few traps you want to dodge from Day One.

Don't Chase "Get-Rich-Quick" Schemes

If someone promises you "double your money in a week" — run.

Real investing takes time. It's boring. It's consistent. It's not flashy or magical.

Easy Peasy Reminder: *If* it sounds too good to be true... it probably is.

Diversify Your Investments

Don't put all your money into one stock—even if it's a "sure thing." Why? Because if that one company tanks, your money tanks with it.

Diversification = Spreading your money across many companies, industries, and even types of investments (like stocks + bonds).

It's like building a team: if one player has a bad day, the rest of your team keeps you in the game.

Understand the Risks: Why Patience Is Key

Investing *always* involves some risk. Your stocks will go up. They will go down. That's normal. The secret is staying calm and sticking with it for the long haul.

Warren Buffett (one of the richest investors ever) said it best:

"*The stock market is a device for transferring money from the impatient to the patient.*" You want to be on the patient side. Always.

Let's Reflect

- Which type of investment sounds most interesting to you: stocks, index funds, or bonds?
- What kind of investor do you want to be—hands-on or autopilot?
- What's one action you can take today to move closer to opening your first investment account?

The sooner you get started—even with a few dollars—the sooner your money can start working harder than you do.

Let's move!

Thinking Long-Term

You've learned *what* investing is and *how* to get started.

Now comes the part that most people—especially young investors—totally mess up.

They think investing is like ordering fast food: you put in $10 today, and by next week, you're rich. Not how it works.

Investing is more like planting a tree.

You water it. You wait. You barely see anything happening at first. But over time, those tiny efforts grow into something massive—strong enough to build your future around.

Let's break it down.

The Difference Between Saving and Investing

Imagine you want to go on a weekend trip with your friends next month. You need about $200. Would you invest your $200 in the stock market, hoping it grows in a month?

No way! You'd save it.

Savings = Short-Term Goals

Investing = Long-term wealth building

Saving is like keeping your money in a safe—it stays there, ready when you need it.

Investing is like sending your money to the gym—it's training to get stronger and bigger, but it needs time to work out.

Easy Peasy Tip

- If you'll need the money within the next year or two, save it.
- If you don't need the money for 5+ years, invest it.

Example: Car vs. Freedom

Let's say you save $5,000 over a few years for a used car. Smart move.

But imagine if you *also* started investing just $20 a month at the same time.

By the time you graduate college, that small investment could have grown into thousands—helping you move out sooner, start a business, or even travel the world debt-free.

Savings = buying stuff soon. Investing = buying your freedom later.

Setting Realistic Investment Goals

Let's be real: you're not going to become a millionaire by investing $5 tomorrow. (If you figure out how, call me.)

But you *can* set simple, realistic goals that build serious wealth over time. Start small—but start smart.

Example Goals for Teens

- Grow $500 into $1,000 in a year by investing consistently.
- Invest $20–$50 a month for the next 2–3 years.
- Build a $2,000 investment account by the time you turn 18.

Easy Peasy Strategy: Milestones

Don't just look at the huge end goal ("I want $100,000!"). Break it into milestones:

- First $100 invested → Celebrate!
- First $1,000 milestone → High five yourself.
- First time you earn dividends → Treat yourself (responsibly).

Real-Life Teen Scenario

Jaden, 16, started investing $25/month from his part-time job walking dogs. After one year, he had about $325 invested. Small, right?

But here's the kicker: He was more proud of that $325 growing in his brokerage account than any $50 gift card he'd ever gotten. It made him feel powerful—because he wasn't just spending money. He was building it.

Small wins fuel bigger wins. Always.

The Importance of Patience

Now, for the hardest but most powerful investing skill of all: **patience. Investing is a marathon, not a sprint.**

It's not about flipping money fast like some TikTok gurus scream about. It's about staying in the game long enough to let your money multiply.

Easy Peasy Analogy

Imagine planting bamboo.

- For years, it looks like nothing's happening—just a little sprout.
- Then suddenly—*BAM!*—it shoots up 90 feet in 6 weeks.
- All that time, the roots were growing underground.

Investing works the same way.

Slow, invisible progress... then massive results if you stay committed.

Real-Life Example

If someone at age 16 invests $50/month into an index fund earning an average 8% return:

- By age 26, they could have around $8,500.
- By age 36, it could be around $25,000.
- By age 46, it could grow to $62,000—even without increasing their monthly investment. (And if they keep adding, it grows even faster.)

All they had to do? Stay consistent and patient. As the legendary investor Charlie Munger said:

"The big money is not in the buying or selling... but in the waiting."

And one more important quote—you've heard it before, but it deserves a spotlight now: "***Time in the market beats timing the market.***"

Trying to predict perfect moments to invest ("I'll wait until the market is low!") is a rookie mistake. Just get in. Stay in. Let time do its magic.

Easy Peasy Reminder

The longer you stay invested, the more powerful your money becomes.

Let's Reflect

- What's one small investment goal you can set today?
- Are you willing to commit to the long-term—even when progress seems slow at first?
- How would future-you (age 25 or 30) feel seeing the results of what you start today?

Habit 6: Key Chapter Takeaway

Investing: The Superpower That Buys Your Future

Let's pause for a second and look at how far you've come.

Last chapter, you learned how to earn active income—trading your time, skills, and energy to make money through side hustles and small businesses. You took control of your finances by saying, "I don't need to wait for some job in the future. I can earn right now."

That's powerful. But here's the truth: you don't want to *work for money* forever. You want to train your money to *work for you.*

That's what investing is.

It's the habit that turns today's hustle into tomorrow's freedom.

This chapter wasn't about picking the hottest stock or chasing some overnight win. It was about building the mindset, skillset, and patience to play the long game—the game most people are too impatient to win.

Let's break it down. You learned that:

- **Investing is one of the best ways to earn passive income—** money that grows even while you sleep.

- **Saving is for short-term goals**, like buying a phone or a car. But **investing is how you build real wealth** that can last for decades.

- You don't need thousands to get started—just a few dollars and the habit of consistency.

- Compound interest is, well, awesome. When you give your money time, it multiplies in ways most people never see coming.

- The key is patience, not perfection. The longer you stay in the game, the stronger your money becomes.

So now the real question is:

How do you turn investing into a habit that sticks?

Just like we've done in every chapter, we use the same CRR formula:

Cue → Routine → Reward

Here's how that works for investing:

- **Cue**: You get paid. Whether it's from babysitting, tutoring, or mowing lawns—you've got some extra income sitting in your account.
- **Routine**: You take action. You transfer a small portion (even just $10 or $20) into your investment account. You choose a stock, index fund, or let your robo-advisor do the work. You don't overthink it—you just stay consistent.
- **Reward**: You watch your money grow over time. You hit your first milestone. You feel more confident, more independent, more in control of your future. And that feeling? That's what makes the habit stick.

Every time you complete that cycle—earn, invest, grow—you're reinforcing one of the most powerful habits anyone can build.

And the best part? You're starting young. That gives you an edge most adults *wish* they had.

You don't need to be rich to invest. But learning to invest is how most people eventually get rich. It's not about luck. It's about long-term commitment.

Every dollar you invest now is a seed for future freedom—freedom to travel, to live on your own terms, to say "no" to jobs or situations that don't align with your goals.

The sooner you start building this habit, the sooner your money becomes more than just something you spend—it becomes something that works for you.

That's the *Easy Peasy way*.

And if you've made it this far, you're already ahead of 99% of people your age. So, let's keep going. You're not just a saver anymore. You're an investor.

And this journey is just getting started.

Interactive Challenges:

Take Control of Your Investing

Part 1: Self-Assessment – What's Your Investment Mindset?

Choose the statement that best describes you:

- **(A)** "I have never thought about investing before—it sounds complicated."
- **(B)** "I'm interested in investing but don't know where to start."
- **(C)** "I've done some research, but I'm not sure if I'm ready to invest yet."
- **(D)** "I already invest (or have tried investing) and want to get better at it."

Reflection: If you chose A or B, take another gander at some of the investing ideas in this chapter. If you chose C or D, you've made a good start, but by adapting some of the lessons here, you'll learn how to make smarter investment choices and grow your wealth.

Part 2: Real-Life Scenario – What Would You Do?

Scenario 6

You just received **$200 for your birthday**, and you want to **grow it over time** instead of spending it right away.

You have **three options**:

1. Put it in **a savings account** where it earns **0.5% interest per year.**

2. Invest it in **a stock market index fund** that historically grows **7-10% per year.**

3. Use it to **buy an expensive item you've been wanting,** thinking you'll save later.

Choose one:

- **(A)** Put all $200 in the savings account—it's safe.
- **(B)** Invest all $200 in an index fund—it has long-term potential.
- **(C)** Spend $100, save $50, and invest $50 for balance.
- **(D)** Look for a way to **earn more money** before investing, so you don't feel short on cash.

Reflection: What choice helps you build wealth over time? How do different options affect your financial future?

Part 3: Investment Challenge – Build Your Investing Knowledge in One Week

Challenge:

Spend **seven days** learning about investing and **take action** by trying **ONE** of the following:

1. The "Investment Tracker" Challenge

- Pick **one** company or stock index (like the S&P 500).
- Track its **daily price movements** for a week.

- **Why?** Helps you **understand how markets move** before investing.

2. The "Start Small" Investment Test

- Use an investment app (like **Acorns, Fidelity Youth, or Greenlight**) to start investing with **$5–$10** (if possible).
- If you're not ready, **pretend to invest** or use a virtual demo trading account and track the amount as if you've bought it but with zero risk.
- **Why?** Helps **build confidence** and makes investing **less intimidating.**

3. The "10-Minute Investing Habit"

- Spend **10 minutes every day** learning about a different investment topic (stocks, ETFs, bonds, compound interest).
- Use **YouTube, podcasts, or articles** to simplify investing concepts.
- **Why?** Learning **a little bit every day** adds up fast!

Reflection:

- Which challenge did you try?
- What did you learn about investing?
- Did this change how you feel about **growing your money**?

Part 4: The Habit Challenge – Build One Investment Habit This Week

Choose **ONE** investing habit below and commit to doing it for seven days:

1. The "Save & Invest" Habit

- Every time you get money (allowance, paycheck, gift), **save 10% and invest 10%.**
- **Why?** Helps you build **long-term wealth** instead of just saving.

2. The "Investing Goal" Habit

- Set a **realistic investing goal** (e.g., invest $50 this month).
- Track your progress and celebrate small wins.
- **Why?** Setting goals makes investing **more rewarding.**

3. The "Investment Research" Habit

- Spend **five minutes daily** learning about **a stock, ETF, or company.**
- Keep a notebook of **what you find interesting.**
- **Why?** The more **informed you are**, the **better investment choices** you'll make.

Reflection:

- Which habit did you choose?

- Did this make investing feel easier and more approachable?
- How will you continue to grow your investments over time?

Part 5: Discussion & Group Activity – The Power of Investing

For Educators, Parents, and Homeschoolers

This section is designed to help teens **understand the power of investing**, recognize its long-term benefits, and develop an investor mindset early on. Through engaging discussions and hands-on activities, they'll explore **how money can grow over time, the risks and rewards of investing, and why starting young gives them a huge advantage**.

Discussion: "What If You Started Investing Today?"

Goal: Help teens visualize how small investments today can turn into big gains over time— and why **starting early matters**.

Discussion agenda:

1. **Think about a time you really wanted something expensive** (a phone, game console, or trip).

- **How long did it take you to save for it?**
- **Imagine you had invested half of that money instead of just saving it.**
- **Use this simple rule:** Money invested in the stock market tends to double every 7-10 years on average.
- **Example:** If you had invested **$100 five years ago**, it could be worth **$150–$200 today!**

- **Would this change how you think about spending vs. investing?**

2. **If you invested just $10 a week, how much could you have in five years?**

   - **Hint:** That's **$2,600 saved**—but invested, it could grow to **$3,000–$3,500 or more!**
   - **What if you started at age 15 versus age 25?**
   - **Why does investing early make such a huge difference?**

3. **Long-term thinking: Would you rather have $1,000 now or $10,000 later?**

   - Why do most people **struggle to wait** for bigger rewards?
   - How can you **train yourself to think like an investor instead of a spender?**
   - **What's one way you could start investing today, even with just a small amount?**
   - **Takeaway: Investing is like planting a tree—the sooner you start, the bigger it grows!**

Activity: "The $100 Investment Time Machine"

Supplies Needed: A pen and some paper, or your phone for calculations

Instructions:

1. **Imagine you invested $100 in the stock market 10 years ago.**

   - Use a simple growth rate of 8% per year (the average return of the S&P 500).

2. Calculate how much it would be worth today.

Use an online **compound interest calculator** or estimate:

- **Year 1:** \$100 → \$108
- **Year 2:** \$108 → \$117
- **Year 3:** \$117 → \$126 (and don't stop there—keep going for 10 years!)

3. Think about your future self.

How much easier would life be if you made small, regular investments—and ended up with \$50,000+ waiting for you in the future?

Discussion:

- Were you surprised by how fast money grows when invested?
- What's stopping most people from investing early?
- How can you make **investing a lifelong habit** instead of something you do "later"?

Takeaway: Your money can work harder than you—if you let it!

Action Habit 6: Become an Investor

The Habit:

Start thinking like an investor by **making your money work for you.**

Daily Action:

- **Save and invest a percentage** of all money you receive.
- Use **free investing apps** to track how markets work.

- Learn about **one new investment concept** each day.

Why It Works:

- Helps you **build wealth early** with minimal effort.
- Teaches **long-term money management skills**.
- Makes investing a **normal part of your financial routine**.

✓ **Challenge:** Set a **small investing goal**, take action, and track your growth over a month!

Habit 6 Progress Check: Did You Take Action?

✓ Quick Review

- Did you complete the Self-Assessment on your investment mindset?
- Did you try one of the investing challenges (Investment Tracker, Start Small Test, or 10-Minute Investing Habit)?
- Did you set a small, realistic investment goal to start building wealth?

✓ Rate Your Progress (1–5 Stars)

★ ★ ★ ★ ★ (How well did you apply today's lesson?)

✓ Action Habit for the Week:

Habit Challenge: Start the "Save & Invest" Habit—every time you receive money, save 10% and invest 10%.

Tip: Track your savings and investment amounts in a simple notebook or an app to see your progress!

Next Step:

Ready to move on? Awesome work! Before moving on, take a moment to reflect:

- What's one thing you learned about investing that surprised you?
- What's your next step in becoming an investor?
- Share your insights with a friend, parent, or teacher!

Alright, take a breath, crack your knuckles—whatever you gotta do. We've got another chapter—and thus another habit—to conquer. Let's keep building your financial future!

Habit 7:

Credit and Debt – How to Borrow Smartly

Credit is like fire: When handled carefully, it warms you. When mishandled, it burns you.

Understanding Credit

Let's be honest: the word "**credit**" doesn't exactly spark excitement. It probably sounds like one of those adult things you'll deal with "someday." But here's the twist—*credit is already a part of your future, whether you're ready or not.*

Want to rent your first apartment? You'll need a good credit score. Buy your first car? You'll need credit.

Even applying for jobs? Yep — employers can check your credit too.

That's why this chapter matters. Because credit isn't just about borrowing money — it's about **building trust**. Think of your credit history like your financial reputation. And the habits you start building now? They're writing the story others will read later.

So, let's talk about what credit really is, how it works, and how to handle it like a boss—before it handles *you.*

What Is Credit and Why Does It Matter?

Credit means borrowing money with the promise of paying it back later. This money could be from a credit card, a student loan, or even that $20 you borrowed from your older sister to grab pizza last Friday. If you borrowed it—and there's an expectation to repay it—that's credit. Got it?

But here's where it gets interesting…

Good credit opens doors. Bad credit locks them shut.

See, with good credit, you're seen as trustworthy. Banks offer you better interest rates, you pay less in fees, and you're more likely to get approved for things that matter—like a car, a house, or even that cell phone contract with unlimited data.

With bad credit, though, you'll face higher interest rates, fewer approvals, and way more financial stress.

So, this isn't just about if you borrow money—it's about how you *repay* it: on time, every time, without missing a beat. It's about staying under your limit, never ignoring your bill, and treating credit like a responsibility—not free money. That's what builds trust. That's what builds *credit.*

Real-Life Teen Scenario

Lucy, 18, got added to her mom's credit card as an authorized user. She decided to only use the card for gas and paid it off in full every month. By the time she turned 21 and applied for her own car loan, she had built up an excellent credit score—and thus qualified for a super low interest rate!

Her friend Ryan, though? He maxed out his first card on a shopping spree, missed a few payments, and ended up paying *thousands more* in interest for the same car. The difference? Not income. Not luck. Just *habits.*

Your Credit Score = Your Financial Reputation

When you borrow money, lenders need to know: "Can we trust this person to pay us back?" And that's where your credit score comes in.

It's a number between 300 and 850 that tells banks, landlords, and even employers how trustworthy you are with money. It's kind of like your GPA—but for your financial behavior.

And just like with school, small habits add up over time. Let's break it down:

How Credit Scores Work

Now, there are **five major ingredients** that go into your credit score:

1. Payment History (35%)

Do you pay your bills on time? This is the biggest factor. One missed payment can hurt your score for months.

2. Credit Utilization (30%)

How much of your available credit are you using? If you have a $1,000 credit limit and you're using $900 of it, that's a red flag. Experts recommend staying under **30%—**ideally even less.

3. Length of Credit History (15%)

The longer you've had credit, the better. That's why starting young—and starting smart—gives you an edge.

4. New Credit (10%)

Every time you apply for a new card or loan, your score dips slightly. As such, applying too often can make you look desperate.

5. Credit Mix (10%)

Lenders like to see that you can handle more than one type of credit (like a credit card plus a student loan). Know why? It shows maturity.

Easy Peasy Analogy

Okay, so imagine your credit score like a trust meter in a video game.

- Paying on time = level up.
- Maxing out your cards = warning lights.
- Paying late = losing XP.

Keep playing smart, and you unlock better rewards—lower interest, better deals, and financial freedom faster.

Good Credit vs. Bad Credit

Let's keep it real: You can have a credit card and still have **terrible** credit. Or you can use credit wisely and build **great** credit over time. It all comes down to how you use it, really.

What Responsible Credit Use Looks Like

- Paying your full balance every month—not just the minimum.
- Keeping spending low (under 30% of your credit limit).
- Only borrowing what you know you can repay—in full.

What Bad Credit Use Looks Like

- Maxing out your card and only paying the minimum.
- Paying late (or not at all).

- Treating a credit card like it's just free money.

And bad credit doesn't just hurt your score. In fact, bad credit habits can cost you big time. We're talking higher prices for everything—car insurance, phone plans, loan approvals—all because lenders don't trust you. Are you starting to get how vital this is?

Where It All Begins: Even Owing $20 Matters

Here's something most teens overlook: **debt isn't just big credit cards and student loans.**

It starts way smaller—like when you borrow $15 from your cousin and forget to pay it back. Or when you owe your parents $50 for last month's concert tickets and push it off for months.

That's why I created the **"Money I Owe"** section inside both **Bonus 2 (Printable Budget Planner)** and **Bonus 3 (Spreadsheet Budget Tracker)**. These tools are going to help you list even the *tiny debts*—the personal IOUs to family and friends—so you never let money damage a relationship—or your own self-respect—ever again!

Easy Peasy Rule

If you owe it, track it. If you borrow it, repay it. And if you're not sure? Write it down and take responsibility.

Make no mistake, your habit of managing small personal debts today becomes the foundation for managing big real-world credit later.

Let's Reflect

- Have you ever borrowed money from someone—even just $10 or $20?

- Did you repay it on time, or did you forget?

- What would it feel like to have people trust you with money—banks, parents, or even future employers?

Once more, good credit is about *trust.* And how is trust built? By doing what you said you'd do—with money, with people, with life. And hey, if you start now, you'll be miles ahead when it's time to apply for your first real credit card, car loan, or apartment.

Now, keep in mind that this isn't about being perfect. It's about being consistent, being responsible, and being the kind of person others (and banks) can trust with a dollar.

Using Credit Cards Wisely

Without a doubt, credit cards can be powerful tools when used with discipline—or, conversely, super dangerous traps when used carelessly. Think of a credit card like a chainsaw: incredibly useful, but only if you know how to handle it!

The Basics of Credit Cards

Alright, let's talk all things credit cards, shall we?

It might sound obvious, but when you swipe your card, what you're doing is spending money that is being borrowed from the credit card company. They pay the merchant upfront—not you. And you know what that means? You owe them back. And if you pay the full amount by the due date? No interest. Zero extra cost. Just convenience and a chance to build credit.

But if you *don't* pay the full amount? That's when interest kicks in—and it kicks *hard.*

- **Interest:** Interest is the extra money you have to pay when you borrow money and don't pay it back right away. It's how credit card companies make money—by charging you an additional percentage of what you actually owe, over and over, every month you don't pay in full. Even small unpaid balances can snowball into big bills if you're not careful.

- **Credit limits**: This is the maximum amount you're allowed to borrow. If your limit is $1,000 and you spend $950, you're almost maxed out. And not that you need me to say this, but that's not too good.

- **Billing cycles**: Credit cards work on monthly cycles. So, you get a statement showing what you spent, and then you have a few weeks to pay it off.

- **Interest rates**: Most cards charge between 15% and 25% interest per year—sometimes more. That means if you leave a $1,000 balance unpaid for a year, you could owe $1,200+.

- **Minimum payments**: Here's the trap. Your statement might say you only have to pay $25 this month. Tempting, right? But paying just the minimum means most of that $25 goes toward paying off the interest only—and not the actual amount you borrowed (which is still due!). So, your debt barely shrinks. And if you keep doing this, you could be stuck paying off the same debt for *years*—with interest piling up far beyond what you originally spent!

- **Pro Tip**: Always pay off your full balance every month. Plain and simple. Just treat your credit card like a debit card with perks.

Avoiding the Debt Spiral

As you can probably tell, credit cards make it incredibly easy to spend money you don't have. And if you're not careful, that small $50 purchase can turn into a $500 headache. Why, exactly? Because of high interest rates. Because of late fees. Because one small mistake becomes a habit. And, frankly, because you never expected it to spiral so quickly.

The Debt Trap in Action: Emma's Story

Emma, 19, got her first credit card in college. It had a $1,000 limit. Her plan was to just use it for textbooks and emergencies.

But then came a weekend concert. And new shoes. And takeout. And another concert. And before she knew it, she'd hit her limit. She figured, "No big deal, I'll pay it off slowly." But she missed a payment. Then she got charged interest. Then she got hit with a late fee.

Long story short, her $1,000 balance? It ballooned to $1,300 in just *two months*. Her parents had to step in, and her credit score took a hit. Later, when she tried to apply for a student apartment, she got rejected because her credit history was already damaged. Emma now has a budget and is rebuilding her credit—but the stress, the embarrassment, and the lost opportunities were all quite real.

And the thing is, Emma's story isn't rare—many teens (and adults!) have and continue to follow suit. So, let this be a wake-up call for anyone who thinks credit is free money!

The Dangers of "Buy Now, Pay Later"

Apps and stores often offer deals like the classic "buy now, pay later." And it sounds great, doesn't it? Get what you want now, worry about the bill later.

But guess what? It's *still debt.* And if you miss a payment? Late fees. Interest. Collections. So, easy rule here: If you wouldn't put it on a credit card, don't "buy now, pay later" either.

Predatory Credit Offers

You know what's especially cruel with credit cards? A lot of companies target young people with bad deals: high fees, low limits, sneaky fine print. On that note, here are some red flags to look out for:

- cards with annual fees but no real rewards
- cards that start with low interest but jump after a few months
- offers that sound too good to be true

So, always read the fine print. Always ask questions. And if you don't understand something, wait until you do!

Responsible Credit Habits

Alright, so how do you use credit cards the *smart* way?

I'm glad you asked! Here's the *Easy Peasy* system:

- **1. The 30% Rule**: Never use more than 30% of your credit limit. If your card limit is $1,000, try not to carry more than $300 at a time. This keeps your credit score healthy.
- **2. Set Payment Reminders**: Use your phone or a calendar. Set alerts a few days before your bill is due. This is because late payments are one of the fastest ways to wreck your credit.
- **3. Use Cards for Essentials Only**: Gas. Groceries. Bills. Stuff you were already planning to pay for. Not impulse buys, gadgets, or clothes you can't afford.

And here's a bonus tip: Use your ***Easy Peasy Budget Tracker*** (Bonus 2 Printable or Bonus 3 Spreadsheet) to stay on top of your credit use. It includes a section for "Money I Owe" so you can track what you've borrowed—from credit cards, parents, or friends!

Seeing it in writing? That's 100% how you stay accountable.

Let's Reflect

- Do you know your credit card's interest rate and payment terms?
- Are you using it for essentials or wants?
- What habits could you start today to keep your credit on track?

The bottom line? Credit cards aren't bad. But using them without a plan is.

Borrowing and Managing Debt

If credit is like fire—helpful when controlled, dangerous when not—then debt is the flame it produces. Too much flame in the wrong place? Things burn down fast. But a steady flame in the right fireplace? That's warmth, light, and progress. See the difference?

Now, let's talk about how to borrow smart, dodge the dangerous traps, and build habits that keep you safe—and thriving—with debt.

Good Debt vs. Bad Debt

Let's clear something up real quick: not all debt is evil. No, I'm not kidding. In fact, some debt can be helpful—kind of like borrowing your pal's bike to get somewhere faster. It's not yours, but you're using it responsibly to move forward. On that note, here are some examples of these two types of debt:

Good debt helps you build your future:

- **student loans** (for education that improves your job opportunities)

- **mortgages** (for buying a home that grows in value)
- **small business loans** (for if you've got a solid plan and future income potential)

Bad debt drags you backwards:

- **high-interest credit cards** (they're used for stuff you don't need)
- **payday loans** (they trap you with outrageous fees)
- **borrowing for fun** (like that $1,000 vacation you're still paying off a year later)

How to Know if Debt Is Worth It

Before you borrow, ask yourself three simple questions:

1. Will this help me earn more money or build something valuable in the future?
2. Can I realistically pay this off—without stress—over time?
3. Is there a cheaper or smarter way to do this (like saving first)?

Real-Life Scenario: Car Loan vs. Saving

Let's say you're 17 and you want a car. Not an unusual tale, right? And then your friend offers to sell you their old ride for $4,000. So, here are your two options:

- **Option A**: Borrow the $4,000 with a high-interest loan. You get the car now, but end up paying $5,000+ after interest. Plus, you're stuck with monthly payments.

- **Option B**: Keep using the bus, save $250 a month, and buy it outright in 16 months—no debt, no interest, no stress.

The lesson here? If borrowing gets you there faster but costs you way more, it might not be worth it.

Understanding Interest Rates

Interest is like the cost of renting money. If you borrow $100 and someone says, "Sure, but you'll owe me $110 next month," that $10 is interest.

And know what can make or break your borrowing decision? Interest rates!

APR = Annual Percentage Rate

This is the fancy name for how much borrowing actually costs you over a year—including interest and any fees. Higher APR equals more money you pay.

Let's break it down:

- **Fixed rate**: Like a flat-fee pizza—same cost every time.
- **Variable rate**: Like surge pricing on ride-shares—changes based on the market. One month it's cheap, next month it's brutal.

Easy Peasy Tip

When comparing loans, don't just look at the monthly payment. Look at the **total cost** over time. Borrowing $1,000 at 25% APR is way more expensive than borrowing it at 8% APR—even if both have the same starting payment.

Pro Move

Always shop around—like you would for a new phone, pair of pants, or concert tickets. Don't accept the first offer. A lower rate means real money saved.

Getting Out of Debt

Already borrowed more than you should have? Hey, it happens. The key is not to panic—it's to *plan.*

Think of debt like a mountain you need to climb down from. And with that image in mind, here are two key ways of bringing that debt down:

- **Snowball it**: Start with your smallest debt first. Pay it off fast to build momentum. Then tackle the next one. It's like rolling a tiny snowball downhill. As it picks up speed, it gains momentum and confidence, helping you crush the next one even faster.

- **Avalanche it**: Start with the debt with the highest interest. Crush that first so you stop bleeding money, then move on to the next highest interest, and so on.

Both methods work and push your debt downhill—one builds momentum, the other saves money faster. So, just pick the one that fits your style more, and stick to it!

Negotiation Tip

Yes, you can negotiate debt. Just call up the company and ask for

- a lower interest rate (especially if you've been paying on time).

- a payment plan you can actually stick to.

- waiving late fees (some do this if you ask nicely and sound serious).

And look, don't be shy. Companies want your money—they'd rather help you pay slowly than not pay at all.

Easy Peasy Reminder

Every smart debt move you make now builds habits that will follow you into adulthood. On that note, think of good debt habits like playing defense in basketball—it's not always glamorous, but hey, it's what wins games.

Let's Reflect

- What's one situation where borrowing might be a smart move?
- Have you ever borrowed something (even from a friend or parent) and had trouble paying it back? What did you learn?
- If you had $1,000 in debt right now, what would your strategy be to pay it off—snowball or avalanche?

Habit 7: Key Chapter Takeaway

Credit is power. But like fire, it depends on how you use it.

By now, you've seen both sides of the coin. Credit and debt can either be your launchpad to independence—or the reason you're stuck, stressed, and spiraling. It all comes down to the **habits you build now**.

This chapter wasn't about fear. It was about **awareness**. Because credit isn't just a piece of plastic or a number on a screen. It's your **financial reputation**. It's how the world decides if it can trust you—with an apartment lease, a car loan, a job, or even a cellphone plan.

And debt? It's not automatically bad. Sometimes borrowing is smart—like a student loan that opens doors. But borrowing without a plan? That's where dreams quietly fall apart.

Let's be real for a moment:

Too many people—even adults—fall into debt traps they can't escape. They swipe without thinking. They pay the minimum. They ignore bills. They let shame pile on top of interest.

Some even lose their homes, their health… their hope. In extreme cases, unmanaged debt has even pushed people toward mental health crises and worse.

That's not meant to scare you—it's a wake-up call. Because it's preventable. And **you're learning now what most people never do.**

Let's break it down.

You learned that:

- **Good credit builds trust.** It saves you money, unlocks opportunity, and sets you apart from the crowd.
- **Bad credit builds walls.** It makes life more expensive, more stressful, and harder than it needs to be.
- **Your habits today shape your financial future.** How you treat money—whether it's $20 borrowed from a friend or $2,000 on a credit card—becomes part of your story.
- **Not all debt is evil.** Some debt moves you forward. Other debt pulls you backward. Learn the difference.
- **There's always a way out.** Whether you snowball or avalanche your way down the mountain, you can beat debt—one smart step at a time.

But knowledge isn't enough.

Like every habit in this book, you need to turn it into action. That's where our ***Easy Peasy CRR Formula*** comes in:

Cue → Routine → Reward: The Credit Habit Formula

Cue: You receive a bill, borrow money, or swipe your card.

It's that moment where your brain says, *"I owe something now."*

Routine: Instead of ignoring it, you take responsible action.

- You check your ***Easy Peasy Budget Tracker*** (Bonus 2 or Bonus 3).
- You make a payment before the due date—in full, if possible.
- You check how much of your limit you've used and stay under 30%.
- You reflect: "Can I really afford this?" before spending another cent.

Reward: You feel calm. In control. Trusted.

Your credit score stays healthy. You avoid fees. You stay out of debt. And most importantly—you're becoming someone who **owns** their financial story.

Every time you repeat that loop—cue, routine, reward—you're writing the habits that will protect you for life.

Here's what I want you to remember:

Credit cards don't ruin lives. Bad habits do. Debt doesn't destroy dreams. Silence does.

You don't need to be rich, or perfect, or some spreadsheet genius to win at credit. You just need to start small, stay aware, and keep practicing the right moves.

So, next time you borrow—from a friend, a parent, or a credit card—ask yourself:

"Can I repay this in full? Am I borrowing to move forward, or just to feel better right now?"

If the answer's clear, you're ready.

And if it's not? That's okay too. Pause. Ask questions. Use your tools.

Because every smart credit move you make today? That's one more reason Future You will say, "I'm so glad I learned this early."

That's the *Easy Peasy* way.

And you're already on your way to being credit-savvy, financially trusted, and debt-free—for life.

Interactive Challenges: Take Control of Your Credit & Debt

Part 1: Self-Assessment – What's Your Credit Mindset?

Choose the statement that best describes you:

- **(A)** "I don't know anything about credit or how it works."
- **(B)** "I know a little about credit, but don't understand how it affects me."
- **(C)** "I understand credit and want to build a good score early."
- **(D)** "I already use credit (or plan to soon) and want to avoid mistakes."

Reflection: If you chose A or B, this chapter will help you **learn the basics of credit and debt.** If you chose C or D, you'll **discover how to use credit responsibly and build a strong financial future.**

Part 2: Real-Life Scenario – What Would You Do?

Scenario 7

You just turned 18 and received an offer for your **first credit card**. It has a **$1,000 credit limit**, and the company offers **0% interest for the first 6 months.**

Your friends encourage you to use it for **a weekend trip that costs $800**, saying you can pay it off later.

Choose one:

- **(A)** Use the credit card to book the trip—it's free money for now!
- **(B)** Use the credit card but only spend $200 to stay within your budget.
- **(C)** Avoid using the card and find a way to save up instead.
- **(D)** Take the credit card but only use it for emergencies or small purchases to build credit.

Reflection: How will this decision impact your credit score, future borrowing power, and financial stress?

Part 3: Credit Challenge – Build Smart Credit Habits in One Week

Challenge:

For **seven days**, focus on learning and practicing smart credit habits by trying **ONE** of the following:

1. The "Credit Report Check" Challenge

- Visit a **free credit score website** (if available in your country) and learn about **what makes up a credit score**.
- **Why?** Helps you understand how lenders evaluate creditworthiness.

2. The "Simulated Credit Card" Test

- Pretend you have a **$500 credit limit** and track imaginary purchases for a week.
- Follow the **30% rule** (never use more than $150).
- **Why?** Helps you **practice responsible credit use** before getting a real card.

3. The "Credit Statement Breakdown"

- Find a sample credit card statement online.
- Highlight the **minimum payment, due date, interest rate, and fees**.
- **Why?** Helps you understand how to avoid late fees and unnecessary charges.

Reflection:

- Which challenge did you try?
- What did you learn about **how credit works**?
- How will this help you make **better financial decisions** in the future?

Part 4: The Habit Challenge – Build One Credit Habit This Week

Choose **ONE** credit habit below and commit to doing it for 7 days:

1. The "Credit Card Safety" Habit

- If you have a credit card (or plan to get one), **set a spending limit** and **treat it like cash.**
- **Why?** Keeps you **from overspending** and helps you **pay off your balance in full.**

2. The "Credit Bill Reminder" Habit

- Set up **a calendar alert** for when a bill is due (even if it's imaginary).
- **Why?** Helps you **build the habit of paying on time**, which is **key for good credit.**

3. The "Good vs. Bad Debt" Habit

- Research **one example of good debt** (e.g., student loans, mortgages) and **one example of bad debt** (e.g., payday loans, high-interest credit cards).

- **Why?** Helps you **understand the difference** and **make smart borrowing choices.**

Reflection:

- Which habit did you choose?
- How did it change your understanding of credit and debt?
- What steps will you take to build good credit and avoid bad debt?

Part 5: Discussion & Group Activity – Understanding Credit & Debt

For Educators, Parents, and Homeschoolers

In this section, educators and parents will guide teens through real-world credit scenarios, critical thinking exercises, and interactive discussions to help them develop smart borrowing habits in a fun and relatable way!

Discussion: "The True Cost of Borrowing"

Goal: Help teens understand how borrowing works and why interest can make debt expensive if not managed wisely.

Discussion agenda:

1. The Cost of "Buy Now, Pay Later" Deals

- Have you ever seen "Buy Now, Pay Later" options when shopping online?
- What do you think happens if someone misses a payment?

Scenario: Imagine you buy a $100 pair of headphones using "Buy Now, Pay Later," but forget to make a payment. The company charges a $10 late fee, and the remaining balance gains interest.

Question: How much do you think that $100 purchase could actually cost after late fees and interest?

2. Why Paying Only the Minimum Can Keep You in Debt

- Let's say you owe $500 on a credit card with an 18% interest rate, and the minimum payment is $20/month.
- **Question:** How long do you think it would take to pay off if you only make minimum payments?

Answer: Over three years—and you'd pay an extra $130+ in interest!

Challenge: Brainstorm ways to avoid long-term debt (e.g., paying more than the minimum, avoiding unnecessary purchases, setting reminders).

3. Good Debt vs. Bad Debt—How Do You Decide?

Scenario: You have two options:

- **(A)** Take out a $5,000 loan for a car that helps you get to work and earn money.
- **(B)** Put $5,000 on a credit card for a dream vacation but have no plan for repaying it.

Question: Which one do you think is good debt, and which is bad debt? Why?

Takeaway: Debt isn't always bad—it's how you use it that matters!

Activity: "The Real Price of Credit"

Supplies Needed: Calculator, sample credit card statement (printed or online), pen C paper.

Instructions

1. Look at a sample credit card statement and identify

- the minimum payment.
- the interest rate (APR).
- the total balance owed.

2. Use an online calculator to see how long it would take to pay off a balance if only the minimum payment is made.

3. Discussion:

- What surprised you the most?
- How much extra do you end up paying in interest?
- What's a smarter way to use credit cards responsibly?

Takeaway: Credit cards aren't free money—they're a tool that must be managed wisely!

Learning how to borrow responsibly will save you thousands of dollars in the future.

Action Habit 7: Become a Credit-Savvy Borrower

The Habit:

Before using credit, always ask yourself: **"Can I afford to pay this off in full by the due date?"**

Daily Action:

- **Learn one new thing about credit** every day (credit scores, interest rates, responsible borrowing).
- **Set a pretend credit limit** and practice using **only a fraction of it.**
- **Talk to a parent or mentor** about their experiences with credit and what they've learned.

Why It Works:

- Helps you build a strong credit history from the start.
- Prevents **debt stress** by promoting **responsible borrowing**.
- Teaches you how to **use credit as a tool, not a trap.**

✓ **Challenge:** Set a **credit goal** (e.g., maintaining a low credit usage, always paying in full) and track your progress for one month!

Tip: If you're thinking about getting a credit card in the future, research different options and **compare interest rates before applying**!

Habit 7 Progress Check: Did You Take Action?

✓ Quick Review

- Did you complete the Self-Assessment on your credit mindset?
- Did you learn about credit scores and how they impact your financial future?
- Did you explore the difference between good debt and bad debt?

✓ Rate Your Progress (1–5 Stars)

★ ★ ★ ★ ★ (How well did you apply today's lesson?)

Next Step:

Ready to move on? Great work! Before moving forward, take a moment to reflect:

- What was your biggest lesson about credit?
- How will you ensure you use credit wisely when the time comes?
- Discuss your thoughts with a friend, parent, or teacher!

Most people spend their whole lives stuck in jobs they hate, stressing over bills, and wondering if freedom was ever meant for them—especially after growing up watching their parents do the same.

But not you. You've learned the core habits—now let's flip the page, and explore what financial freedom really means, and how to start building it long before adulthood chains you into a 9-to-5.

Habit 8 (Bonus):

Financial Independence – Building Habits for Life

Financial independence isn't about being rich—it's about being free to live life on your terms.

Welcome to Bonus Habit 8! Yep, you heard that right—*bonus*. You already learned the seven core habits that most adults wish they'd mastered as teens. And now? You're unlocking the first of two powerful extra habits designed to give you the kind of financial edge that sets you apart from the crowd.

This is your reward for showing up, sticking with it, and committing to your future. And what better bonus than this one?

Financial Independence

It sounds big. It sounds bold. And honestly? It's what all the other habits were secretly building toward.

So what is it, *really*?

Let's break it down—the *Easy Peasy* way.

Defining Financial Independence

What Does Financial Independence Look Like?

Financial independence *isn't* about yachts, gold chains, or retiring at 25 so you can live on a beach drinking coconut smoothies (though hey, no judgment if that's your thing).

It's about one thing: **freedom**.

Freedom to choose the kind of work you want to do—not the job you're stuck with just to pay bills. Freedom to travel when you want, help your family when needed, or say "no thanks" to a paycheck that doesn't respect your time or talent.

It's about having options.

Not being trapped. Not being stressed. Not saying "I can't afford it" every time life throws you an opportunity.

Think of it like this:

Being financially independent is like driving your own car instead of being stuck on a school bus. No waiting. No random stops. You go where you want, when you want.

Now, here's the part most people skip over—the engine that makes this freedom possible.

Financial independence happens when your **passive income** is far greater than your **monthly expenses**. That means even if you don't work another day in your life, your rent is paid. Your groceries are covered. Your Netflix subscription? Yep, still streaming.

Because your money is working for you… even while you sleep. Let's make this real.

Imagine this:

You wake up on a random Tuesday morning. You're in a 5-star hotel in Dubai. It wasn't even planned — just a spontaneous trip you booked last-minute because you *felt like it.* Your flights? Covered. Your hotel? Covered. Your meals, clothes, and gym membership back home? Covered.

And guess what? You're not stressed. You're not hustling. You're not checking your bank balance every three minutes.

Because you don't need a paycheck to survive—your investments, royalties, side hustle income, or other passive income streams are already doing the heavy lifting all on autopilot.

That's not fantasy. That's freedom.

The moment your monthly **income on autopilot** far exceeds your **monthly bills**, the game changes.

Work becomes a choice—not a chore. You're the boss of your time. You're not just living life… you're designing it.

And the journey to get there?

It starts here—with the habits you're learning in this book.

The Role of Habits in Achieving Independence

Now, here's the plot twist:

Financial independence isn't a switch you flip when you hit 30. It's a snowball—built slowly, one habit at a time.

Saving $1 a day might not sound exciting. But do it every day for a year, and you've got $365. Now imagine investing that yearly savings for 10 or 20 years. With compound growth, that tiny snowball turns into a financial avalanche—in the best way.

Compound growth is when your money starts earning money… and then that money earns *more* money. It's like planting a tree that grows fruit — and each fruit has seeds that grow into more trees.

It all starts with the habits you're building right now:

- budgeting before buying
- saving before spending
- earning outside your job
- investing early
- thinking before swiping
- saying "no" to stuff you don't need
- saying "yes" to your future self

These habits? They aren't just about surviving. They're about stacking wins that build freedom.

Let me give you a real-life story.

Real-Life Teen Scenario: Meet Sophie

Sophie started side hustling at 16—selling digital art online. She saved half her earnings, invested in index funds by age 18, and lived below her means even after landing a high-paying job at 22. By the time she was 27, she had enough invested to walk away from her job—not because she had to, but because she *wanted* to. She now freelances part-time, travels the world, and spends most of her time mentoring other young creators.

No magic. No lottery. Just smart habits started early.

What Financial Independence Is NOT

Let's clear up a few common myths.

It's not about being a millionaire overnight.

No crypto jackpot. No sketchy courses promising "five-figure months." Just boring, beautiful, consistent growth.

It's not about quitting work forever.

It's about working on your terms. Maybe you love your job—great! Financial independence just means you're never stuck doing something you *don't* love.

It's not avoiding responsibility.

It's owning your life. All of it.

And before we go further, let's reintroduce two important terms (from Habits 5 and 6) that will help you build that life:

Active Income vs. Passive Income

Active income remember, is what you earn by trading your time for money. Babysitting, waiting tables, coding websites. Clock in, get paid. Clock out, no pay.

Passive income is money that automatically comes into your pocket whether you're working or not. Like…

- dividends from investments.
- royalties from books or music.
- rent from a property.
- ad revenue from a YouTube channel you built once and now earns while you sleep

Passive income is the engine of financial independence. When your passive income covers your monthly expenses? Ding ding ding! You've hit financial freedom.

And that, my friend, is what we're building here.

Let's Reflect

- What does *your* version of financial independence look like?
- If money weren't a problem, what would you spend your time doing?
- What's one area of your life today where money limits your choices—and how would that change if you had financial freedom?
- Do you want to work for money forever, or have money work for you?

Sustaining Habits Into Adulthood

Consistency Is Key

Here's a truth bomb no one tells you: becoming financially independent doesn't happen in a single big leap — it happens one boring, consistent habit at a time.

It's like brushing your teeth. You don't skip it just because you're tired, right? (Okay… maybe once or twice. But still.) You do it because you're aware of the long-term payoff: clean teeth, no cavities, and not scaring people away with your dragon breath.

Money works the same way. It's not about a "big win"—it's about small habits, repeated forever.

Let's say you set up an automatic savings transfer—$50 a month from your checking account into savings. That's not flashy. No one's posting it on TikTok. But over time, that tiny action becomes your safety net, your travel fund, your startup seed money.

Same with investing. The earlier you automate your investments—even if it's just a few bucks a week into an index fund—the more your money works for you, not the other way around. That's compound growth. That's money earning money while you go off and do your thing.

But here's the kicker: *life changes.*

You graduate high school. Move to college. Get your first job. Start adulting (ugh). Suddenly, your budget is juggling rent, groceries, student loans, maybe even your own Netflix account.

So, what do you do?

You adapt—but you don't quit!

Real-World Scenario

Meet Alex. At 19, he got a job at a local electronics store, earning $1,200 a month. After rent, food, and gas, he had about $250 left. Instead of blowing it on stuff he didn't need, he split it: $100 into savings, $75 into investments, and $75 for fun.

Six months in, guess what? He had $600 saved, his investments had grown a bit, and he still enjoyed the occasional gaming night and pizza run.

That's not luck. That's *consistency.*

Easy Peasy Tip

Treat your budget like a fitness plan — it needs to adjust as life changes, but the routine should never disappear.

Financial Checklists for Milestones

Okay, let's talk life milestones—the big moments where money suddenly matters more than ever.

We're talking about

- buying your first car.
- renting your first apartment.
- traveling without mooching off your parents.
- starting your own business.
- even saving for retirement (yeah, that starts earlier than you think!).

So, let's deal with these milestones by employing a basic "financial to-do" list to start hitting as early as possible:

- Build a 3–6 month emergency fund (for when life throws a curveball).
- Keep your credit score strong (remember Habit 7!).
- Create a budget for rent, bills, and groceries—not just vibes.
- Start investing a small percentage of your income (even if it's $20/month).
- Avoid high-interest debt like it's a zombie bite.

And here's the secret sauce:

Review your plan every year.

Why? Because once again, life changes! Maybe you switch majors. Or your side hustle takes off. Or you fall in love with someone who has a wildly different money mindset than you.

Just like you wouldn't wear the same shoes every year, don't walk into new life stages with the same old plan. Review. Adjust. Improve.

Building Multiple Income Streams

If financial independence is your destination, then income streams are the highways that get you there. And spoiler alert: you need more than one.

Relying on a single paycheck is like riding a bike with one wheel — fine until you hit a bump.

That's where multiple income streams come in.

Let's break it down one more time:

- **Active income** = you work, you earn. That's your job, your tutoring gig, your babysitting money.
- **Passive income** = money you earn without constantly working for it. Think: rental income, dividends, selling digital products, or creating a YouTube channel that keeps paying you months after you uploaded.

Real-Life Teen Scenario

Jade, 17, started selling stickers on Etsy from designs she made on her iPad. She made $40 the first month, then $120, then *$250*. Now, she gets sales even when she's sleeping! That's passive income in action—her digital art working overtime.

Here are a few teen-friendly side hustles and income ideas:

- Freelance skills (design, writing, video editing)
- Selling digital products (printables, ebooks, stock music)

- Starting a YouTube or TikTok channel and monetizing it
- Offering tutoring in subjects you're strong in
- Starting a blog or a small online store

Not sure where to start? Feeling overwhelmed by the list above? You're not alone. Most teens don't talk about it, but the fear of failure is real. You might be thinking: *What if I mess up*? I'm too afraid to take the first step. What if I'm not good enough to pull it off?

But here's the truth: everyone starts scared. The only difference between those who succeed and those who don't? are the ones who try anyway. Start small. Start messy. But just start.

Pick the idea that feels easiest, most exciting, or closest to something you already enjoy. Don't overthink it—just try the one that feels doable. The goal isn't to go viral — it's to get moving.

***Easy Peasy Rule*:** Start with one. Make it work. Then add another.

The goal? Build a life where your bills are paid before you even roll out of bed. That's not a fantasy—that's financial independence in action.

Let's Reflect

- Are you saving and investing on autopilot?
- What financial milestone are you most excited (or nervous) about?
- Can you think of one skill you could turn into a side hustle this year?

Stay consistent. Keep checking your progress. And remember: Financial freedom isn't a finish line—it's a lifestyle. Start shaping it *now*.

Avoiding Common Pitfalls

If building financial independence is like hiking up a mountain, then this section is about not tripping over your own shoelaces and stumbling backward. Because here's the truth: Even with great habits, the wrong mindset or a few bad choices can quietly pull you off track.

With that in mind, let's look at the three biggest potholes—and how to avoid falling into them.

Dealing With Lifestyle Inflation

Here's the classic trap: you *earn* more money, so you start *spending* more money.

It makes sense in your head: "I've worked hard, so I deserve this upgrade." Right? But if you're not careful, your new lifestyle eats every dollar of your raise—and suddenly, you're back to square one.

This is called **lifestyle inflation**, and it's a sneaky one. It looks like

- upgrading to a more expensive car the second you get a better paycheck.
- buying designer clothes instead of sticking to your budget.
- going from microwave ramen to fancy sushi four nights a week.

Real-Life Teen Example

Meet Greg. At 17, he got a part-time job that paid him $500 a month. His friends started flexing their new kicks and flashy tech. Instead of joining the spend-fest, though, Greg set a goal: to save up for a used car by the end of the year.

He still hung out with friends, of course, but he skipped the $9 lattes and impulse fashion buys. And a year later? While his friends were still Ubering around with empty wallets, Greg bought his first car—*in cash.*

Moral of the story: Just because your paycheck grows doesn't mean your spending should.

Recognizing Money Mistakes Early

Look, everybody makes money mistakes. The trick isn't to be perfect—it's to **catch the mistake early** before it snowballs.

So, here are a few red flags to watch for:

- You've stopped checking your budget.
- You're using credit to cover fun purchases—not emergencies.
- You're saving "whatever's left over"… and surprise—nothing's left.

Ignoring small money mistakes is like ignoring a tiny leak in your ceiling. It doesn't feel urgent… until your whole room is soaked!

Let's say you spent your rent money on a new gaming console. At first, you might think, "No problem, I'll just cut back next month." But then next month comes… and so do interest fees, late penalties, and awkward convos with your landlord or parents.

Lesson: When your financial gut says, "This might be a bad idea"—*listen.*

Better yet? Do monthly "Money Health Checks." Just sit down for 10 minutes and ask:

- *Did I overspend anywhere this month?*
- *Am I saving and investing consistently?*
- *What did I do well, and what can I improve?*

Pro Tip: If you want an easy way to check in with your money each month, grab your free **Bonus 2 Printable Budget Planner** or **Bonus 3 Spreadsheet Tracker**. Inside, there's space to track your income, savings, spending, and even the little IOUs you owe to friends or family.

It's like a monthly financial mirror—it won't lie, but it *will* help you see what's working and what needs adjusting.

Staying Motivated Through Setbacks

Here's the part most financial books don't tell you: Sometimes life hits you with a curveball.

- You lose your job.
- Your laptop breaks right before finals.
- An unexpected bill drains your savings.

When these moments hit, it's easy to feel like you've failed. But you haven't—you've just hit a detour. Setbacks don't mean you're off track… that is, unless you quit.

That's why the most powerful tool you can build is **resilience—**the ability to bounce back, learn from the hit, and keep going.

How?

Well, first off, start with a **small emergency fund**. Even $200 stashed away can make the difference between a crisis and a speed bump.

And second? **Celebrate your small wins**.

You saved $50 this month? Awesome. You made your first side hustle sale? That counts. You finally canceled that useless subscription you forgot about? Huge win.

The point is, teens who stay motivated through setbacks don't do it by accident. They create **systems**—simple routines that keep them moving forward even when life gets messy.

Easy Peasy Recap

- **Earning more ≠ spending more.** Avoid lifestyle inflation and remember Greg's story.
- **Small mistakes become big problems if ignored.** Catch them early, like financial cavities.
- **Setbacks are part of the journey.** Build a cushion, bounce back, and celebrate progress.

Bonus Habit 8: Key Chapter Takeaway

Financial independence isn't about flexing. It's about freedom.

You've made it through Bonus Habit 8—your first free bonus chapter for going above and beyond. This chapter wasn't just "extra content." It's the *real endgame*. Because everything you've learned so far—from saving and budgeting to spending and investing—was leading here.

Financial independence is the moment your money works harder than you do. Where your *passive income* (investments, royalties, digital products, rental income — all that good stuff) earns more than your monthly bills. *That's* when you stop surviving and start designing your life.

Let's recap what you've just learned across all three sections:

You defined what financial independence really means.

It's not about becoming a millionaire overnight or quitting work forever. It's about *options*.

It means waking up on a random Tuesday in a Barcelona hotel room, knowing your bills are covered whether you decide to open your laptop or not. Why? Because your money—not your time—is funding your lifestyle.

You understood that real financial freedom starts when your **passive income outpaces your active income**, giving you the power to choose when, where, and how you want to work (or not work at all!).

You learned how to sustain your good habits into adulthood.

Financial independence doesn't happen from one lucky break. It happens because you:

- stay consistent with saving and investing (even when life gets messy).
- adjust your plan as you grow (college, first job, big dreams).
- build *multiple* income streams that don't rely on a single paycheck.

You now know that a little money invested early beats a lot of money invested late—and that budgeting and long-term planning is your financial gym. The more reps you do, the stronger you get.

You discovered how to avoid the traps that stop most people.

You saw how easy it is to fall into *lifestyle inflation*—earning more but spending it all on shinier stuff. You learned how to spot financial mistakes before they blow up. And most importantly, you know how to bounce back from setbacks with small wins and solid routines.

You found out that setbacks don't ruin dreams. Quitting does.

Cue → Routine → Reward: Your Financial Freedom CRR Habit Formula

This book isn't just about facts. It's about *habits*—repeatable actions that stack over time to build wealth, confidence, and freedom.

Here's how that habit loop plays out in real life:

Cue

You get paid. Or you see something you want. Or you get hit with a bill. These are your *financial cues*—little triggers that could lead to smart choices… or not.

Routine

Instead of reacting, you follow your financial independence routine:

- You send money into savings automatically.
- You invest before you spend.
- You check your budget instead of winging it.
- You say "no" to what doesn't align with your goals.
- You track progress in your Budget Planner (hello, Bonus 2 and 3!).

Reward

You feel calm. Confident. In control. Your future gets clearer. Your bank account grows. And one day—without even realizing it—you wake up to find *you're free.*

You've crossed that invisible line where work becomes a choice, not a necessity.

Words of Wisdom From Noah

Look—I'm not here to promise yachts and private jets.

But I *am* here to promise this:

If you build the right money habits now, you will *never* be stuck in a life you didn't choose.

You will never have to stay in a job that drains you.

You will never panic when the bills hit.

And you *can* live your version of the Dubai lifestyle—humbly, freely, and fully—because you put in the work today to give Future You options.

So, ask yourself:

- What does my "freedom life" look like?
- What passive income streams excite me?
- What habit can I lock in today to move one step closer?

Then go do it.

Because financial independence isn't reserved for rich adults in suits.

It's built by smart teens who start early—like you.

Let's do this!

Interactive Challenges:

Take Control of Your Financial Independence

Part 1: Self-Assessment – What's Your Financial Independence Mindset?

Choose the statement that best describes you:

- **(A)** "I haven't thought about financial independence—I just spend what I have."
- **(B)** "I want to be financially independent, but I don't know where to start."
- **(C)** "I already save and budget but need to learn about growing my money."
- **(D)** "I have a financial plan and want to stay on track long-term."

Reflection: If you chose A or B, that's okay—that's what this chapter's been written for: helping you **understand the foundation of financial independence**. And if you chose C or D, you'll **learn how to sustain and expand your financial habits for lifelong success**.

Part 2: Real-Life Scenario – What Would You Do?

Scenario 8

You just received a **paycheck of $500** from your part-time job. You want to **enjoy some of it**, but you also have **long-term financial goals** like saving for a car and investing.

Choose one:

- **(A)** Spend the full $500 on fun—you'll start saving later.
- **(B)** Save $400 and only spend $100 on things you enjoy.
- **(C)** Split it evenly: $250 for fun, $250 toward savings and investments.
- **(D)** Invest part of it, save part of it, and use part of it to start a side hustle.

Reflection: Which choice sets you up for **both short-term enjoyment and long-term financial success**? What would a financially independent person do?

Part 3: Financial Independence Challenge – Build Future Wealth in One Week

Challenge:

For seven days, focus on developing habits that lead to financial independence by choosing **ONE** of the following:

1. The "Future Budget" Challenge

- Plan a **hypothetical monthly budget** as if you were financially independent.
- Include expenses, savings, investments, and fun money.
- **Why?** Helps you visualize financial freedom and make adjustments now.

2. The "Multiple Streams of Income" Challenge

- Brainstorm **three ways** you could make money outside of a regular job (side hustle, passive income, freelancing).
- Research one and create a simple action plan.
- **Why?** Learning **how to generate income beyond a paycheck** is key to financial independence.

3. The "Minimalist Week" Challenge

- Cut unnecessary expenses for a **full week**—no impulse spending, no unnecessary subscriptions, no eating out.

- Track how much you save.
- **Why?** Helps you identify spending habits that don't align with your financial goals.

Reflection:

- Which challenge did you choose?
- What did you learn about your financial habits?
- How will you apply these lessons to build long-term wealth?

Part 4: The Habit Challenge – Build One Financial Independence Habit This Week

Choose **ONE** financial habit below and commit to doing it for seven days:

1. The "Pay Yourself First" Habit

- Before spending money, **automatically transfer a set percentage into savings or investments**.
- **Why?** Ensures you prioritize your future self over short-term wants.

2. The "Long-Term Vision" Habit

- Write down **one major financial goal** (e.g., buying a car, traveling, retiring early).
- Research how much it costs and create a **mini financial roadmap** to achieve it.
- **Why?** Helps you **think long-term and stay motivated**.

3. The "Track & Adjust" Habit

- Review **your weekly spending** and see where you can cut back or invest more.
- Make a small change to improve your financial future.
- **Why?** Regularly adjusting keeps your money aligned with your goals.

Reflection:

- Which habit did you choose?
- Did it make you feel **more in control of your financial future**?
- How can you continue this habit long-term?

Part 5: Discussion & Group Activity – The Path to Financial Independence

For Educators, Parents, and Homeschoolers

This section helps teens think critically about financial independence and how small daily decisions impact their long-term financial future. Through discussions and engaging activities, teens will visualize their financial future and develop habits for lifelong wealth-building.

Discussion: "What Does Financial Independence Mean to You?"

Goal: Help teens define financial independence in a way that's meaningful to them and understand how to work toward it.

Discussion agenda:

1. Financial Freedom vs. Financial Struggles

- What does financial independence look like to you? (Example: Traveling, owning a home, starting a business, retiring early?)
- What are some things that could prevent someone from becoming financially independent?
- How do early financial habits help prevent financial struggles later in life?

2. Earning Money While You Sleep

- What is passive income, and how is it different from a paycheck?
- If you could create one source of passive income, what would it be? (Examples: Owning a business, investing, selling digital products)
- Why do financially independent people focus on earning in multiple ways instead of just working a job?

3. Your Future Self: What Would You Say?

- Imagine you're 10 years older and you've achieved financial independence.
- What advice would Future You give to your present self about money?
- What's one habit you can start today to move closer to financial freedom?

Takeaway: Financial independence isn't about luck—it's about making smart choices today that give you freedom tomorrow!

Activity: "The 10-Year Financial Vision"

Supplies Needed: Notebook, pen, and a calculator (optional).

Instructions:

1. Imagine your dream lifestyle 10 years from now. Close your eyes for 30 seconds. Picture it. What does financial freedom *feel* like? Where are you living? What do your days look like? Who's around you? What do you get to say yes to—and what do you no longer worry about?

Write down:

- Where do you live?
- What kind of job (or business) do you have?
- How much money do you need each month to cover your expenses?

2. Break it down into goals:

- How much money would you need to save or invest yearly to achieve this lifestyle?
- What are 2–3 ways you could increase your income over time?

3. Plan your first step:

- What's **ONE** small thing you can start doing this week to get closer to this vision?

Discussion:

- Did anything surprise you about your future financial needs?

- How can you make sure you're in control of your money, not the other way around?
- What habits do you need to build now to set yourself up for success?

Takeaway: Financial independence is achievable with small, consistent actions—your future self will thank you for starting early!

Action Habit 8: Become Financially Independent

The Habit:

Start thinking and acting like a financially independent person **now**.

Daily Action:

- **Set a financial goal** and break it into actionable steps.
- **Automate savings** so you're always building your future.
- **Find ways to earn outside of a paycheck** (side hustles, investments, passive income).

Why It Works:

- Helps you **gain financial freedom faster** by developing the right mindset and habits.
- **Keeps you focused on long-term success rather than short-term spending.**
- Builds **confidence and control over your financial future**.

✓ **Challenge:** Set a **one-year financial independence goal** and track your progress each month!

Habit 8 Progress Check: Did You Take Action?

✓ Quick Review

- Did you complete the Self-Assessment on your financial independence mindset?
- Did you explore ways to create multiple income streams?
- Did you reflect on how small financial habits impact your long-term financial future?

✓ Rate Your Progress (1–5 Stars)

★★★★★ *(How well did you apply today's lessons?)*

Next Step:

Ready to move on? Take a moment to reflect:

- What was your biggest insight about financial independence?
- How will you make sure your money is working for you instead of just working for money?
- Discuss your thoughts with a friend, parent, or teacher!

You've made some amazing progress. Just one more bonus chapter to go—let's do this!

Habit 9 (Bonus):

Building Wealth With Technology – Digital Currency, AI, and Future Trends

The future of money is here. Are you ready for it?

Welcome to *The Main Event.*

You've already mastered the seven foundational money habits, and you've unlocked the first bonus—building financial independence. But this chapter? Our final outing together?

This is where everything changes. This is where we shift gears and dive headfirst into the world of technology—the future of money, work, income, and everything in between.

Because here's the truth that most people never hear until it's too late: The world is going *cashless.* AI is replacing jobs faster than anyone expected. And the traditional rules of "work hard, retire at 65, live off your pension" are quietly crumbling.

But while most adults are panicking, you have an edge.

You're here. You're learning. And Bonus Habit 9 right here is your chance to future-proof your finances and build wealth in a way your parents never could.

Think of this chapter as your early access pass to the economy of the near future.

We're going to talk about digital currency, artificial intelligence, and new money-making opportunities that most schools don't teach and most teens never even hear about. You'll learn how to use AI to earn, budget, and invest—not to mention how to protect yourself in a world filled with opportunity and risk!

But before we go any further—let's address something important: Relying on a job alone isn't a plan. It's a *gamble.*

See, AI is already reshaping industries that used to be considered safe:

- Legal research is now handled by software.
- Accounting tasks are done by AI faster and cheaper than humans.
- Self-driving cars are edging out drivers.
- Even creative jobs like design, content writing, and music production are being transformed by AI tools.

And at the same time, governments across the world are drowning in national debt, struggling to pay pensions and healthcare bills for aging populations. The safety nets that existed for past generations? They're full of holes.

Long story short, the system will not save you.

But believe it or not, that's not bad news—it's your cue to *take control.*

And to help you do that, keep in mind that you're also getting *Bonus 4: The Easy Peasy AI Wealth Guide for Teens*—a free downloadable guide filled with tools, apps, real-life teen case studies, and interactive challenges to help you turn AI into your personal wealth-building assistant. You'll learn how teens just like you are using tech to freelance, invest, and even launch small digital businesses from home.

Just scan the QR code in this book to grab your free copy.

With that said, though, let's get moving with the current chapter and find out just how digital money works—and then how to use it *wisely.*

Understanding Digital Currency

What Are Cryptocurrencies?

Imagine a world where there are no paper bills, no coins, no big lines at the bank, and no government printing more money whenever it runs short. That's where cryptocurrency comes in.

Cryptocurrencies like **Bitcoin**, **Ethereum**, and others are essentially a new kind of money. But instead of being printed by any specific government, they're created and tracked through **blockchain technology**—a giant, secure digital ledger that records every transaction ever made and is not bound to any particular country.

Think of it like a magical notebook shared with the whole world. Once you write something in it, it can never be erased or changed—and everyone can see it. That's how blockchain makes crypto so secure and trustworthy, even without a bank in the middle.

Cool, right?

Now, here's a lightning-fast guide to the specific crypto out there:

- **Bitcoin** is the OG, of course. It was created in 2009 as a peer-to-peer digital currency.

- **Ethereum** came next—it's like Bitcoin's younger sibling, but with extra superpowers. It allows people to create apps and contracts that run automatically on the blockchain.

- And then there are thousands of other cryptocurrencies too, and these are typically called "altcoins." Not to just toss all these aside completely, but it's worth knowing that most are either copycats, experimental, or… scams (but we'll get to that).

So, why does this matter to you, exactly?

Because governments and major banks around the world—from the US to China—are now starting to build their own **digital currencies**, called Central Bank Digital Currencies (or CBDCs for short). What does this mean, then? Two things: First, that crypto is not a fad, and second, that cash, as we know it, may be gone in your lifetime.

This shift is like moving from DVDs to streaming, but bigger. Much bigger. And once you go digital, there's simply no turning back. But here's the catch: Crypto can be **super risky**—especially for teens who don't understand it fully. Why's that? Because prices go up and down like a roller coaster on jet fuel. One social media post can crash a coin's value. One hack can wipe out your entire account. And because it's still new, scammers lurk *everywhere.*

That's why we'll always say this:

Only invest what you can afford to lose.

Crypto might be part of the future, but it's not your magic golden ticket. Use it to learn. Use it wisely. But don't bet the farm.

Digital Wallets Made Easy

Let's say you want to dip your toes into the crypto world. You'll need a **digital wallet**. Think of it like your online piggy bank, except it holds coins made of code.

There are two types of wallets:

- **Hot Wallets** (online): Apps like Coinbase or Trust Wallet—easy to set up, perfect for beginners, but slightly more vulnerable to hacks.

- **Cold Wallets** (offline): Hardware wallets like Ledger—super secure, but better once you have more to protect.

Setting one up is often as simple as downloading an app, creating a password, and writing down a "seed phrase" (your backup key).

Whatever you do, don't lose this phrase—it's like the one key to open your digital vault!

Real-Life Teen Scenario

Meet Ray, 16. He took online surveys that paid in Bitcoin (sites like Bituro and Timebucks offer these options). And after a month, he'd earned $100 in crypto and transferred it to a digital wallet. His next step? Learning how to store it safely and track its value.

Avoiding Crypto Scams

Now for the not-so-fun part: scams.

Crypto is like the Wild West—filled with gold, but also with bandits. So, some common traps to watch out for include the following:

- **Fake giveaways**: "Send us 0.1 Bitcoin, and we'll send you back 1 Bitcoin!" (Spoiler: You won't get anything back.)
- **Pump-and-dump schemes**: In short, influencers hype up a coin they secretly own, the price goes up, they sell, and you're left holding a worthless bag.
- **Phishing**: Fake emails or DMs asking you to log into your crypto account… and then, you guessed it, stealing your info.

So, what's your defense?

1. **Do your homework.** If you don't understand how a coin works, don't touch it.
2. **Verify sources.** Never trust a DM from a "crypto expert" you don't know.
3. **Start small.** Begin with tiny amounts. Learn the ropes first.

4. **Use this rule**: Only invest what you can afford to lose—like play money. Because sometimes… it disappears like magic.

AI and Money Management

It's safe to say that artificial intelligence is no longer just a feature from some sci-fi fantasy movie where robots take over the world. No, sir. Today, AI is present everywhere. And instead of taking over the world (well, depends on how you look at it!), it's helping people manage their money, grow their wealth, and even choose better investment strategies—all from a smartphone.

But okay, let's break this down into bite-sized pieces. Because if used wisely, AI can absolutely become one of the most powerful money tools in your financial toolbox.

How AI Can Help You Save and Budget

Imagine this: you've got a personal finance coach that never sleeps, doesn't judge you for your spending habits, and reminds you (nicely) when you're about to blow your pizza budget for the third time this week.

That's what modern AI budgeting apps do. Not bad, right?

Apps like **Cleo** or **Mint AI** connect to your bank account, study your income, track your expenses, and then—here's the magic—they start giving you personalized advice. Cleo, for example, talks to you like a sarcastic best friend. She'll roast you if you spend too much on fast food, then challenge you to save $50 this week.

Even **ChatGPT** can answer your money questions. Not sure how compound interest works? Just ask. Confused about credit scores? Ask again. Look, you've got 24/7 access to financial knowledge that used to take hours of research or expensive coaching! You're growing up in an amazing time, it must be said.

Real-Life Teen Scenario

Meet Taylor. She's 15, works a weekend job at a local café, and constantly runs out of money halfway through the month. Then she connected her bank account to a budgeting AI app. In no time at all, it flagged her impulse buys and showed her how she could save $75 a month just by cutting back on small purchases. Over four months, she saved $300—money she used to buy a new tablet for school. And she didn't have to track anything manually!

Lesson: AI won't save money for you—but it *will* show you where to tighten the belt and where your habits need tweaking.

AI and Investing

Okay, let's bring investing into this. You remember investing, right—the part where your money starts doing pushups while you sleep?

But hang on, what if you don't know *where* to invest? Or how much risk is too much? That's where AI steps in again, wearing a business suit and tie this time.

Robo-advisors are automated investing platforms like **Wealthfront** or **Betterment**. You tell them your goals (like saving for college or buying a car), and they create a personalized investment plan using fancy algorithms that analyze risk, returns, and market conditions. Then they manage everything for you—rebalancing your portfolio, reinvesting dividends, and adjusting to market changes—with zero emotional decision-making, to boot. It's like hiring a money manager, minus the high fees and awkward coffee meetings.

AI also helps you research individual stocks, ETFs, or sectors. See, tools powered by AI can scan thousands of data points in seconds, giving you insights that used to require a finance degree. Even beginner-friendly apps now offer "AI investment suggestions" based on your spending, savings, and goals.

Real-Life Teen Scenario

Fred, 16, saved $400 from a summer job. Instead of guessing where to invest, he used a robo-advisor to create a balanced portfolio. A year later, he was up 9%—without lifting a finger. No charts. No stock tips from TikTok influencers. Just quiet, consistent growth through automation.

Takeaway: AI doesn't replace learning—but it *does* reduce guesswork. It's your copilot, though, not your autopilot. You still need to check your dashboard.

Jobs in the AI Revolution

Let's face it: AI isn't just changing how we manage money—it's changing how we *earn* it.

While it's true that AI is replacing some traditional jobs (like cashiers, telemarketers, and even some legal or accounting roles), it's also creating entirely new ones—and you're still early to the party!

The winners? Teens who learn the skills AI can't easily replace: **creativity, coding, critical thinking, problem-solving, and adaptability.**

On that note, here are a few **teen-friendly career paths** exploding thanks to AI:

- AI prompt engineers (writing smart questions to guide AI responses)
- Data analysts
- Coders and app developers
- Digital artists (yes, even AI-generated art needs humans)
- AI tool freelancers (using AI tools to write, design, edit, and research)

Skills You Can Learn Now

- **Coding** (Python is a great place to start)
- **Data analysis** (free tools like Excel, Tableau, and Google Sheets can help)
- **Content creation** using AI-enhanced tools
- **Automation and chatbot building** (No-code tools like Zapier or Make)

Real-Life Teen Scenario

Nina, 17, started using AI tools to help businesses rewrite product descriptions faster. She offered this as a service on Fiverr. In three months, she earned over $1,000—all by using free AI tools and her own writing flair!

Moral of the story? The AI economy is wide open—but only to those who are paying attention and learning the skills that matter. The earlier you start, the bigger the head start.

Let's Reflect

- Are you using any AI tools already to manage your money or time?
- What skills do you already have that could be boosted by AI?
- Which career paths or side hustles in the AI space sound exciting to you?

See, in the future, it won't just be about how hard you work. It will be about how smart your tools are. And if you're the one building, using, or selling those tools? You'll always be in demand.

Preparing for the Future

The world is changing—*fast.* What worked for your parents financially might not work for you. Heck, what worked *five years ago* might already be outdated. This section, then, is going to be all about future-proofing your finances, your skills, and your safety. Because in a world where technology changes overnight, the smartest teens aren't just reacting—they're *preparing.*

Let's future-proof your money, the *Easy Peasy* way.

How Money Is Changing

Picture this: You walk into a store, grab a snack, tap your phone on the card reader, and walk out. No coins. No bills.

And hey, maybe you already do that. Plenty of people do. But that's because we're living on the brink of a **cashless society**.

Countries like Sweden are even further ahead of us when it comes to achieving this cash-free paradise. Even vending machines take cards these days. And digital payments through Apple Pay, Google Wallet, and crypto wallets are becoming the new normal. In fact, some stores don't even accept cash at all anymore!

What does this mean for you? It means that digital literacy—knowing how to manage money online, track transactions, and stay secure—is now just as important as knowing how to do basic math. Not kidding.

It's like this: if financial literacy is learning how to ride a bike, then **digital financial literacy** is learning how to ride a smart bike with GPS, Bluetooth, and self-parking mode. Same principles, new tools. With me so far?

And if you're not keeping up? Well, I'm sorry to say, but you're falling behind—not just in tech, but in life choices, job opportunities, and income streams.

Teens today need to understand how to

- move money digitally.
- track spending online.
- protect their identity and assets.
- spot digital scams.
- use AI-powered tools wisely.

This isn't optional anymore. It's essential. And luckily, this book—and your habits—are already preparing you for it.

New Income Streams for the Digital Age

Let's talk side hustles—and not the "sell candy bars at school" kind (though, hey, respect if you ever did). We're talking **digital side hustles** that can scale, grow, and pay while you sleep.

There's a whole new economy out there, and teens are already crushing it in ways that didn't exist 10 years ago.

Here's just a taste:

- **NFTs** (non-fungible tokens): Digital art, collectibles, and music being bought and sold using crypto. Not a quick-win scheme, but a creative gold mine if you know your stuff.
- **Freelancing**: Writing, video editing, design, coding—if you've got a skill, someone's willing to pay for it.
- **Digital products**: Printables, templates, ebooks, online courses, stock music, YouTube intros… the list is endless.
- **Online content**: Blogs, YouTube channels, TikTok, and Instagram Reels—platforms where attention equals income.

Real-Life Teen Scenario

Meet Jacob, 16. He started a TikTok page making short, funny videos about study tips and school hacks. He used AI tools to edit faster and started posting daily. One video went viral. Then another. And then within four months, he'd built 80K followers and launched a $9 digital study planner. He sold *600 copies*. That's **$5,400 in sales—**from a hobby, not a job.

Now? He's investing the profits and building a brand. All because he started—and he kept at it.

The lesson? **Your online presence can become your digital storefront.** And if you build it with purpose and value, it pays you back.

So, no—you don't need millions of followers. What you *do* need is consistency, creativity, and the courage to try.

Staying Safe Online

Alright, now for the not-so-fun-but-100%-necessary part: staying safe in a digital world.

That's right: As your digital income, assets, and online activity grow, so do your risks. Cyber scams are like mosquitoes in summer: always buzzing, always trying to bite.

Here's what you need to know:

- **Phishing scams**: Fake emails or messages pretending to be from your bank, school, or a tech company. They try to trick you into clicking shady links or giving away your password. Don't. Just don't.

- **Fake crypto giveaways**: "Send us $100, we'll send back $1,000!" Spoiler alert: You'll never see that $100 again.

- **Too-good-to-be-true job offers**: "Make $5K/week from home!" If it sounds too good to be true… Well, you already know.

What to do instead:

- Use **strong, unique passwords—**no more "1234" or "password1"
- Enable **two-factor authentication** (yes, it's annoying, but it *works*)
- Keep your devices updated—old tech equals easy access for hackers!
- Don't click on sketchy links or download files from strangers (basic survival rule of the internet, really)

Ultimately, your identity and your money are worth protecting. Guard them like you would your phone—or your snacks.

A Reality Check (And a Pep Talk) From Me to You

The future isn't waiting.

- AI is already taking over jobs—even the "safe" ones.
- Governments are stretched thin—and pensions may not be there when you retire.
- The job market? Crowded and unstable.
- The school system? Still teaching outdated lessons while TikTok creators are building six-figure businesses from their bedrooms.

But don't panic. Why?

Because you're not behind—you're ahead.

See, most teens never read books like this.

Most teens never think about financial freedom, passive income, or digital futures.

Most teens never even get the chance to learn these things before the real world smacks them in the face.

But you? You've got this guide. You've got nine life-changing habits. And you've got time. That's your real advantage.

So, let's finish strong:

- Don't wait for your parents or teachers to figure out the new rules.
- Don't sit around hoping the government has a plan.
- Don't sleep on your potential because you think you're "just a teen."

The future belongs to the bold — and to those who build habits that last.

Don't fear the change. Embrace it. Master it. And lead it.

Because this chapter wasn't just about money. It was about taking control of your life—in a world that's changing faster than ever.

Bonus Habit 9: Key Chapter Takeaway

You've just unlocked one of the most powerful chapters in this entire guide—and not because it was packed with buzzwords like crypto, NFTs, or artificial intelligence.

No—it's because this chapter showed you a truth that most people—especially adults—are still trying to ignore:

The rules of money are changing. Fast.

Paper bills are fading. Jobs that once felt safe are being automated. Governments are deep in debt and struggling to support aging populations.

In short: **no one's coming to save you.**

But here's the hope:

You don't need saving—not if you build the right habits now.

Let's recap what you just learned:

You Understood Digital Currency

You learned that **cryptocurrencies like Bitcoin and Ethereum** aren't just internet money—they're part of a bigger global shift toward **cashless societies** and decentralized finance.

You saw how **digital wallets** work like online piggy banks. You learned the difference between a hot wallet and a cold wallet. You even met teens earning Bitcoin for simple tasks like surveys.

But I also warned you:

Crypto can be risky.

For every kid who earned $100, there's another who lost it all in a scam.

The habit lesson?

Don't chase shiny coins—chase smart habits.

Learn first. Start small. And remember the golden rule: Only invest what you can afford to lose.

You Explored AI and Money Management

You discovered that AI is more than just robots or chatbots—it's your **digital sidekick** for budgeting, saving, investing, and even earning online.

- You saw how apps like **Cleo and Mint** can help you track spending and save money automatically.
- You explored **robo-advisors** that invest for you, stress-free.
- You met teens using AI tools to freelance, launch gigs, and earn real money.

The lesson?

AI won't do the work for you. But it will make you work smarter.

So, what habit do we build here?

Good question. My answer? You should **use AI like a flashlight—**to spot leaks in your budget, growth in your investments, and income you didn't even know you could earn.

You Prepared for a Digital Future

You saw what's really coming:

- **Cashless societies** where physical money is replaced by taps, QR codes, and crypto wallets.
- **New income streams** powered by digital products, freelancing, and content creation.
- And a **digital job market** where AI is both a threat and an opportunity—depending on whether you're learning… or ignoring.

You also saw the risks: phishing scams, fake giveaways, and job-replacing algorithms. But now? You know how to protect yourself.

The habit?

Stay alert. Stay adaptable. Stay building.

Cue → Routine → Reward: Your Digital Wealth CRR Formula

Every great habit starts with a cue—something that triggers action.

Cue: You get paid. You hear about AI. You spot a new digital trend.

Routine: Instead of scrolling or spending blindly, you

- use an AI app to track your spending.
- invest a percentage in a robo-advisor.
- start a low-risk side hustle online.
- secure your passwords, check your financial plan, and adjust monthly.

Reward: You wake up with more options. More money. More *control.*

All in all, you're not just working for money. Your money—and your tech—is working for you. *That's* real freedom. And that's how teens build wealth in a world where grown-ups are still guessing.

Again, AI isn't here to replace you. It's here to *empower* you—if you're willing to learn and adapt, that is. And if you want help with that? Don't forget to check out your free *Bonus 4: The Easy Peasy AI Wealth Guide for Teens.*

Inside, you'll find

- tools and apps to build income.
- AI money challenges and easy-to-follow AI prompts.

- case studies of real teens using AI to freelance, create content, and launch side hustles.
- safety tips to keep your data and identity secure.
- a vision for what AI-powered wealth looks like for your generation.

Just scan the QR code and dive in.

Interactive Challenges:

Mastering the Future of Money

Part 1: Self-Assessment – How Ready Are You for the Future of Money?

Choose the statement that best describes you:

- **(A)** "I don't know much about digital money or AI, and it seems confusing."
- **(B)** "I've heard of cryptocurrency and AI, but don't know how it applies to me."
- **(C)** "I've used digital wallets, investing apps, or AI tools before and want to learn more."
- **(D)** "I actively use digital currency, AI budgeting tools, or invest online and want to stay ahead of new trends."

Reflection: If you chose A or B, this chapter will **help you understand the basics of digital finance**. Whereas if you picked C or

D, it'll help you **learn just how to maximize technology for financial success.**

Part 2: Real-Life Scenario – What Would You Do?

Scenario 9

Let's say you just received **$100 as a gift**, and instead of spending it immediately, you want to explore **future financial trends** like AI budgeting, investing, or cryptocurrency.

Choose one:

- **(A)** Deposit it into a savings account like always—it's the safest option.
- **(B)** Use an AI budgeting app to track how you spend and save the $100.
- **(C)** Invest a portion into a beginner-friendly robo-advisor or stock index fund.
- **(D)** Buy a small amount of cryptocurrency and learn how digital wallets work.

Reflection: How could different **technology-driven financial tools** help you **grow your money instead of just spending or saving it?**

Part 3: Future Money Challenge – Try a Digital Money Tool for One Week

Challenge:

For seven days, explore how technology can help you manage money better by choosing **ONE** of the following:

1. The "AI Budgeting" Challenge

- Download and test a budgeting app with AI features (e.g., Cleo, Mint, or YNAB).
- Track your expenses and see what insights the AI gives you.
- **Why?** AI tools can help automate your financial habits and uncover spending patterns.

2. The "Investing Simulation" Challenge

- Use a stock market simulator or demo trading account to **pretend-invest** $1,000.
- Track your investments daily and note how market changes affect your returns.
- **Why?** Helps you understand how investing works without real risk.

3. The "Crypto Exploration" Challenge

- Research and create a plan for how **you would buy and store cryptocurrency safely**.
- Look into beginner-friendly crypto platforms (e.g., Coinbase, Binance) and understand how digital wallets work.
- **Why?** Prepares you for the growing digital economy without making risky investments.

Reflection:

- Which challenge did you choose?

- What did you learn about **using technology for financial growth**?
- How can you continue **exploring digital finance trends**?

Part 4: The Habit Challenge – Build One Future-Focused Financial Habit This Week

Choose **ONE** habit below and commit to doing it for seven days:

1. The "Digital Money" Habit

- Set up and start using a **secure digital wallet** (even if just for learning).
- **Why?** Prepares you for **cashless payments and digital transactions.**

2. The "Tech-Savvy Earning" Habit

- Explore **one way to earn money online** using AI, freelancing, or digital products.
- **Why?** Helps you future-proof your income by adapting to new trends.

3. The "Online Security" Habit

- Strengthen **your online financial security** by updating passwords, enabling two-factor authentication, and avoiding suspicious links.
- **Why?** Protecting your **financial identity is just as important as growing your money.**

Reflection:

- Which habit did you choose?
- Did it **make you feel more confident** in using technology for money?
- How can you **continue integrating digital finance tools into your life**?

Part 5: Discussion & Group Activity – The Future of Wealth & Technology

For Educators, Parents, and Homeschoolers

This final discussion challenges teens to think critically about the future of money and how technology will shape their financial success. It helps them connect everything they've learned in the book to real-life opportunities and prepares them to stay ahead in a digital world.

Discussion: "How Will You Use Technology to Build Wealth?"

Goal: Help teens understand how AI, digital money, and technology can give them a financial advantage when used wisely.

Discussion agenda:

1. What's the Most Exciting Thing About the Future of Money?

- What financial technologies are you most excited about? (AI, investing apps, digital currency, online businesses, etc.)
- What future career or money-making opportunities do you think will exist that don't even exist today?

- How can you start preparing now to take advantage of these opportunities?

2. Technology vs. Traditional Money Habits

- Do you think AI budgeting apps can replace traditional budgeting? Why or why not?
- If you could choose between cash, a debit card, or cryptocurrency for everyday spending, which would you use and why?
- How can you balance using digital financial tools without becoming too dependent on technology?

3. Your Future Financial Plan: Staying Ahead of the Game

- Imagine yourself in 10 years—how do you think you'll earn, spend, and invest money?
- What's one tech-related financial habit you plan to continue for life?
- How can you stay educated and adaptable as new financial trends emerge?

Takeaway: Technology is constantly evolving, and so is the world of money. The more you learn and adapt, the more financially powerful you become.

Activity: "Your Future Finance Blueprint"

Supplies Needed: A notebook and pen, or, optionally, access to a budgeting or investing app.

Instructions:

1. Your Digital Money Plan:

- If you were given $1,000 today, how would you invest, save, or use technology to make it grow?
- Would you put it in crypto, AI-managed investments, a side hustle, or a savings account?

2. Your Future Job & Earning Plan:

- What type of job or digital income would you like to have in 5–10 years?
- What skills do you need to start learning now to succeed in the digital economy?

3. Your Financial Security Plan:

- How will you protect your financial future?
- What security measures will you take to avoid scams, fraud, or bad investments?

Discussion

- What surprised you about your financial blueprint?
- How will technology help you reach your financial goals faster?
- What's one action you can take this month to get started?

Takeaway: Your financial future is in your hands. Technology gives you new tools and opportunities—but the key is to use them wisely and stay ahead.

Action Habit 9: Become a Future-Ready Money Expert

The Habit:

Stay ahead by **learning and adapting to financial technology trends**.

Daily Action:

- Try **one new digital money tool** each month (AI budgeting, investing apps, crypto research).
- **Follow tech and finance trends** to stay informed.
- Build **digital income streams** (freelancing, online business, investing).

Why It Works:

- Helps you **stay financially relevant** in a changing world.
- Gives you **early exposure to digital money habits**.
- Prepares you for **future financial independence.**

✓ **Challenge:** Set a **six-month goal** to master **one aspect of digital finance** (investing, AI budgeting, or earning online) and track your progress!

Habit 9 Progress Check: Did You Take Action?

✓ **Quick Review**

- Did you complete the Self-Assessment on your readiness for the future of money?
- Did you explore a digital finance tool like AI budgeting, investing apps, or cryptocurrency?
- Did you reflect on how technology can help you build wealth smarter and faster?

✓ **Rate Your Progress (1–5 Stars)**

★★★★★ (How well did you apply today's lesson?)

Your journey doesn't stop here! Keep learning, keep growing, and keep building your financial knowledge, practicing smart money habits and staying ahead of the game. Your future self will thank you!

Conclusion:

You Did It! Now, Let's Make It Stick

If you've made it to this page—pause and give yourself a serious high-five.

No, really. You just read an entire book about money, habits, and building the life you want. That's not "normal" teen behavior (in the best way possible). You've officially done what most adults *still* haven't.

So let's take a moment to look at everything you've achieved—and how to keep it going.

Quick Recap: The Nine Habits That'll Change Your Life

You didn't just read some random finance tips. You built a system—a toolbox of powerful habits designed to help you **save, spend, earn, and grow** with confidence.

Here's what's now part of your DNA:

1. **Mindset**: You shifted from "I can't" to "How can I?" and started thinking like a money-maker.

2. **Saving**: You learned how to plant money seeds and grow them into freedom.

3. **Spending Smart**: You've ditched the dopamine traps and mastered the art of mindful choices.

4. **Budgeting**: You took control of your money and told it where to go.

5. **Earning**: You discovered that income is a skill, and you're ready to level up.

6. **Investing**: You peeked into the future and learned how to make your money grow while you sleep.

7. **Debt Smarts**: You now know how to avoid the traps that wreck most people's futures.

8. **Bonus Habit – Financial Independence**: You're building freedom habits *today*—not in some far-off future.

9. **Bonus Habit – The Future of Money**: You've got your eyes on AI, crypto, and the digital tools that are reshaping the world.

That's not just a list. That's a *lifestyle.*

Cue → Routine → Reward: The CRR Habit Formula That Got You Here

Remember this golden CRR loop?

You've seen it in action throughout this book. Back in Habit 1, Tony used it to get fit. You used it to build up your budgeting muscle. And now it's the secret formula that will keep your new money habits on autopilot long after you close this book.

Example

- **Cue**: You get paid.

- **Routine**: You budget, save a portion, then enjoy your "fun fund."

- **Reward**: You feel confident, in control, and on track toward your goals.

The more you loop this formula into your daily life, the more unstoppable you become.

Why I Wrote This Book... Continued

I started off this book by telling you a bit about why I wanted to write it. Well, as we wrap up, I really want to go over some of that reasoning again. See, when I was your age, I simply didn't *have this*. No one sat me down and said, "Here's how money works. And here's how to build the kind of life you actually want". I had to figure it out through trial, error, and a whole lot of expensive mistakes. So, I wrote this for you because—I've been where you are. I've felt that mix of confusion, frustration, and curiosity. And I want you to have something I never did: *a head start.*

You now have the tools. More importantly, you have the *willingness.* And that puts you ahead of 95% of the world already. But don't stop here. Don't let this be just another book you read and forget about. Let it be the first spark in a fire that fuels your entire future.

A Final Word From Me to You

I want you to hear this loud and clear:

You should be proud.

This book was never about being perfect with money. It's about *showing up*, *learning*, and *building habits* that most people avoid because they're "too boring," "too hard," or "not urgent."

But not you.

You *invested* in yourself—and that decision alone already puts you miles ahead. Your future self? You're going to look back and say, "Wow, I'm so glad I started when I did."

So, whether you're saving your first $100, building your first side hustle, or investing your first dollar in the stock market—I'll say this:

Keep going. Don't wait for the "perfect" moment. *Just start.*

Okay… Hold Up!

Before we part ways, I have to ask:

- **You sure you've actually read through the entire book?**
- **You didn't skip chapters did you?**
- **What if you didn't fully finish or fully engage with the book…?**

If so, no shame here.

Maybe you skipped a few sections. Or perhaps, your parents or teacher asked you to read this, but your heart wasn't really in it. That's okay!

But here's the real question:

Did you give yourself a fair shot to build at least one money habit you can actually use?

If not, here's what I suggest:

- **Pick one chapter that feels relevant to where you're at right now** (saving, earning, spending less, whatever). Start fresh—just that one.

- **Use the self-assessment at the end of the challenges** to score your progress. Aim for at least a 4 out of 5. If you hit it—awesome. If not, take your time and begin round 2.

- **Once you've nailed one habit, come back for another.** This book isn't going anywhere.

You don't need to read every single word to get something powerful out of it. But you do need to take *one step* that gets you closer to where you want to be.

Because trust me—your money habits won't change by accident. But they *can* change with just a little effort, one week at a time.

What Happens Next?

Here's what I recommend:

- **Review your highlighted sections across each chapter that speak to you most**—quotes, tips, stories, or challenges. These are parts that resonated with you personally.

- **Keep this book close**. Every few weeks or months, revisit your highlights to refresh your thinking and reinforce your habits.

- **Re-read your favorite chapter every few months**—see how far you've come.

- **Keep using the five free bonuses** (budget tools, AI guide, discussion toolkit—you've got it all!).

- **Pick one habit to focus on this week. *Just one.*** Don't try to do it all. The goal is momentum, not perfection.

- **Share what you've learned.** Teach a sibling, a friend, or even your parents. Teaching something is the best way to master it.

Final Challenge

I promise it's a quick one!

Grab a notebook (or just pull out your phone).

Write down this sentence:

"The #1 habit I'm committed to building this month is..." (and, you know, write down the habit.)

Now, say it out loud. *Own it.* Then get to work!

Let's Wrap Up!

Picture this: You, a few years from now.

Debt-free. Earning money while you sleep. Taking random trips to Dubai "just because." Spoiling your parents. Spoiling your dog. Maybe even helping out some charitable efforts in your community that you care about.

That's not fantasy. That's the reward of starting young.

"The best time to start was yesterday. The next best time is today."

Today, you started. Now keep going. Keep learning. Keep growing.

And if the world ever tries to convince you that "you're too young" or "it's too hard"—remember this: You've already begun. And that means you're already ahead.

Stay sharp, stay hungry, stay humble.

I'll be rooting for you every step of the way.

–Noah Hawkins

Thank You for Reading!

First, **thank you for purchasing this book**—I truly appreciate it. I know there are plenty of teen finance books out there, so the fact that you chose this one means a lot.

One Last Favor...

If this book helped you (or your teen) build stronger money habits, I'd love for you to leave a quick review. It takes just 60 seconds, and it helps more readers discover this guide, learn these skills, and avoid the mistakes we all wish we'd known earlier.

Simply scan the QR code below or visit the Amazon page to share your thoughts.

Your support helps me continue creating resources that empower teens—and yes, I read every review. It means a lot, truly.

Thank you again for being part of this journey. With gratitude,

Noah Hawkins

My Next Book

The Only DBT Skills Workbook for Teens You'll Ever Need

7 Easy DBT Steps to Transform Anxiety, Stress & Toxic Habits into Calm, Confidence & Unshakable Resilience for Life

This interactive, therapist-level workbook takes you step by step through the 7 essential DBT skills trusted by clinicians worldwide. It's written just for teens — no fluff, no boring therapy-speak, and no endless box-checking.

Instead, you'll get:

- Real tools to manage intense emotions like anger, anxiety, or sadness
- Powerful strategies for setting boundaries and repairing relationships
- Exercises to break destructive habits like self-harm, avoidance, and impulsivity
- A full emotional roadmap to help you build confidence, clarity, and long-term resilience

If Money Skills helped you master your wallet, this one will help you master your mind.

Releasing Mid-Autumn 2025

Book 3: Launching Early 2026

Also, watch out for the next instalment in the Easy Peasy Series — The Easy Peasy Guide to Growth Mindset for Teens, releasing early 2026.

About the Author

Noah Hawkins is a passionate educator, youth mentor, and advocate for teen personal growth and financial literacy. With a background in psychology and behavioral sciences, he specializes in helping young people build smart money habits and long-lasting personal routines—whether around money, mindset, or emotional well-being—that genuinely stick for life.

Noah has worked with teens and young adults through workshops, community programs, and online resources that are focused on budgeting, saving, earning, and investing. His approach is practical, relatable and rooted in habit science—breaking down complex financial topics into clear, easy-to-follow lessons.

In this way, he strives to empower teens to take control of their money with a healthy dose of clarity and confidence.

Drawing on his own struggles as a teen—overthinking, financial stress, and little guidance—Noah is deeply committed to teaching real-world life skills that schools often skip. Whether he's teaching about money, resilience, or mental clarity, his goal is to help teens take control of their future with clarity, courage, and confidence.

When he's not writing, Noah enjoys traveling, hiking, and journaling. He lives in the suburbs of Chicago with his wife, Meredith, and their two kids, where he continues to research teen behavior and financial trends to help the next generation reach all their unique goals.

Glossary of Financial Terms

Below you'll find pretty much all the key money terms used throughout this book. Feel free to use it to review or refresh your understanding at any point!

A

Active Income – Money earned through direct effort or work, such as wages, salary, or freelance jobs.

Allowance – A set amount of money given regularly, often by a parent or guardian, to teach money management and responsibility.

Amortization – The gradual repayment of a loan over time through scheduled payments that cover both principal and interest. It's common with mortgages and car loans.

APR (Annual Percentage Rate) – The total yearly cost of borrowing money, including interest and fees, expressed as a percentage. APR helps compare the true cost of loans or credit cards.

Asset Class – A category of investment that shares similar characteristics. Common asset classes include stocks, bonds, real estate, and cash. Diversifying your investments across different asset classes can help manage risk.

Assets – Items of value owned by a person, such as cash, savings, property, or investments.

Automation – A system that automatically moves money into savings or investment accounts without requiring manual action.

B

Balance – The amount of money currently available in a bank account or owed on a loan or credit card.

Bank Account – A secure account provided by a financial institution for storing and managing money.

Bank Statement – A document provided by a bank that lists all transactions in an account over a specific period, including deposits, withdrawals, and fees. It's used to track account activity and verify balances.

Blockchain – A digital ledger technology that records transactions across a network of computers. It's best known as the foundation of cryptocurrencies like Bitcoin and Ethereum.

Bond – A type of investment where you lend money to a government or company for a set period of time. In return, they agree to pay you interest and return your money later. Bonds are often considered lower risk than stocks.

Borrowing – Receiving money from a lender with the agreement that it will be paid back, usually with interest.

Budget – A financial plan outlining expected income and expenses over a specific period of time.

Budget Deficit – When expenses exceed income during a specific period, resulting in a negative balance. It's the opposite of a surplus.

Budget Surplus – When income is greater than expenses, leaving extra money that can be saved, invested, or used for other goals.

C

Cash Flow – The movement of money in and out of a person's account, reflecting income and expenses.

Checking Account – A type of bank account used for daily spending, deposits, and withdrawals.

Collateral – An asset pledged as security for a loan.

Compound vs. Simple Interest – Compound interest is calculated on the original amount (principal) plus any interest already earned—allowing money to grow faster over time. Simple interest is calculated only on the original amount, without compounding.

Compound Interest – Interest calculated on both the initial principal and the accumulated interest from previous periods.

Credit – The ability to borrow money now and repay it later, typically with interest.

Credit Card – A card issued by a bank that allows purchases using borrowed money.

Credit Limit – The maximum amount a person can borrow on a credit card.

Credit Report – A detailed record of your credit history, including loans, payment history, credit inquiries, and outstanding debts. It's used by lenders to assess creditworthiness.

Credit Score – A numerical rating that reflects a person's creditworthiness based on their borrowing and repayment history.

Credit Utilization Ratio – The percentage of your available credit that you're using. It's a major factor in your credit score. Lower ratios (ideally below 30%) are considered better.

Cryptocurrency – A digital form of money that uses encryption and blockchain technology.

Currency – A system of money used in a country or region to exchange goods and services. Common examples include the U.S. dollar (USD), the British pound (GBP), and the Euro (EUR).

D

Debt – Money owed to another party, typically as a result of borrowing.

Deduction – An amount subtracted from income or a paycheck, often for taxes or benefits.

Default – The failure to repay a loan or meet the terms of a credit agreement. Defaulting can damage your credit score and lead to legal or financial consequences.

Deposit – Money placed into a bank account.

Depreciation – The reduction in the value of an asset over time, often due to wear, age, or obsolescence. It's commonly used when referring to cars or equipment losing value.

Direct Deposit – An electronic transfer of funds directly into a bank account, usually from an employer.

Disposable Income – The amount of money left over after paying taxes and essential expenses. It's what you can spend or save freely.

Diversification – A strategy of spreading investments across different assets to reduce risk.

Dividend – A portion of a company's profits that is distributed or paid to shareholders, usually in cash or additional shares on a regular basis (monthly, quarterly, annually, etc.), as a reward for their investment.

E

Emergency Fund – Savings set aside to cover unexpected expenses such as medical bills or urgent repairs.

Entrepreneur – A person who starts and operates a business, often taking on financial risks.

Equity – The value of ownership in an asset, such as a home or business, after subtracting any debts.

ETF (Exchange-Traded Fund) – A type of investment fund that holds a collection of assets—such as stocks or bonds—and trades on stock exchanges like a regular stock. ETFs offer diversification and often have lower fees than mutual funds.

Expenses – Money spent on goods and services, including both essential (needs) and nonessential (wants) items.

F

Fair Value – The estimated worth of an asset based on its current market price, condition, and expected future value. It represents a reasonable price that both buyer and seller agree on under normal conditions.

Fee – A charge for a service, often found in banking, investing, or financial transactions.

Fiat Currency – Government-issued money that is not backed by a physical commodity like gold. Its value is based on trust in the government that issues it (e.g., USD, EUR, GBP).

FICO Score – A widely used type of credit score developed by the Fair Isaac Corporation, ranging from 300 to 850. It's based on credit report data and helps lenders evaluate risk.

Financial Goal – A specific target for how money will be saved, spent, or invested over time.

Financial Literacy – The ability to understand and apply financial concepts such as budgeting, saving, and investing.

Fixed Expense – A recurring cost that remains constant, such as rent or a subscription fee.

G

GDP (Gross Domestic Product) – The total value of all goods and services produced within a country during a specific period. It's used to measure a nation's overall economic performance and health.

Grace Period – A set period during which a borrower can pay back a loan or credit card balance without being charged interest or penalties.

Gross Income – The total earnings before deductions—such as taxes or insurance—are taken out.

Gross vs. Net Income – Gross income refers to the total earnings before any deductions. Net income, in contrast, is what's left after deductions like taxes and insurance (this is also called take-home pay).

H

Habit Loop (Behavioral Concept) – A pattern of behavior consisting of a cue (trigger), a routine (action), and a reward (result). Understanding this cycle can help build positive money habits and break unhelpful ones.

I

Identity Theft – When someone illegally uses another person's personal or financial information.

Income – Money received, typically on a regular basis, from work, allowances, gifts, or investments.

Inflation – The rate at which prices for goods and services increase over time, reducing purchasing power.

Inflation Hedge – An investment or asset that helps protect against the decreasing value of money due to inflation, such as real estate, commodities, or inflation-protected securities.

Inflation Rate – The percentage increase in prices over time, showing how quickly the cost of goods and services is rising in the economy.

Installment Loan – A loan repaid over time with a set number of scheduled payments, such as a car loan or student loan.

Interest – The cost of borrowing money or the return earned on savings and investments.

Investment – The act of allocating money into assets such as stocks, mutual funds, or businesses with the goal of generating income or appreciation over time.

J

Job Market – The availability of employment and labor, often influenced by economic conditions.

L

Liability – Any legal financial debt or obligation owed to another party.

Liquidity – How easily an asset can be converted into cash without losing value.

Loan – A sum of money borrowed that must be repaid, usually with interest.

M

Minimum Payment – The smallest amount that must be paid on a credit card or loan each month to avoid penalties.

Mobile Banking – Managing bank accounts through apps or websites using a smartphone or tablet.

Money Mindset – A person's beliefs and attitudes about money, shaped by experience and environment.

Mutual Fund – An investment fund that pools money from multiple investors to buy a diversified portfolio of stocks, bonds, or other assets. Managed by professionals, mutual funds aim to reduce risk through diversification.

N

Needs vs. Wants – A budgeting principle that distinguishes between essential expenses (needs) and nonessential purchases (wants).

Net Income – The amount of money left after deductions from gross income; also called take-home pay.

Net Worth – The total value of what you own (your assets) minus what you owe (your debts or liabilities). A positive net worth means you own more than you owe; a negative net worth means you owe more than you own.

O

Overdraft – When you spend more money than is available in your bank account, resulting in a negative balance. This often incurs fees unless you have overdraft protection.

P

Passive Income – Earnings received with little or no active involvement, such as rental income or dividends.

Pay Yourself First – A saving strategy where you automatically set aside money for savings or investing before spending on anything else.

Prepaid Card – A reloadable card funded with your own money, often used as an alternative to cash or credit cards. Helps teach budgeting and spending control.

Principal – The original amount of money borrowed or invested, not including interest.

PSHE – *Personal, Social, Health and Economic education.* A subject taught in UK schools that helps students develop life skills, financial literacy, relationships, and emotional wellbeing.

R

Rainy Day Fund – A small amount of savings reserved for minor unexpected expenses.

Recession – A significant decline in economic activity across the economy, typically lasting for at least two consecutive quarters. Recessions can lead to job losses and reduced consumer spending.

Return on Investment (ROI) – A measure of how much money is earned (or lost) from an investment compared to the original amount invested.

Robo-Advisor – A digital platform that provides automated financial planning and investment services using algorithms.

S

Salary – A fixed regular payment, typically paid monthly or biweekly by an employer.

Saving – Setting aside money for future use instead of spending it immediately.

Savings Account – A bank account designed for storing money securely while earning interest.

Scam – A dishonest scheme intended to trick people out of money or personal information.

SEL – *Social and Emotional Learning.* A U.S. school framework that helps students understand and manage emotions, set goals, show empathy, and build healthy relationships.

Share – A single unit of ownership in a company or investment fund. Shares represent a portion of a business or asset that investors can buy or sell.

Side Hustle – A secondary job or activity that generates extra income in addition to one's main job or school.

SMART Goal – A framework for setting goals that are in line with the acronym "SMART"—meaning goals that are specific, measurable, attainable, relevant, and time-bound.

Spending Plan – Another term for budget; a strategy for managing how income is used.

Stock – A type of investment that represents partial ownership in a company. When you own a stock, you own a share of that company and may benefit from its growth and profits.

Student Loan – A type of loan designed to help cover education-related expenses.

T

Taxes – Mandatory financial charges imposed by the government on income, goods, and services.

Time Value of Money – The idea that money available today is worth more than the same amount in the future due to its earning potential.

Transaction – Any activity involving money moving in or out of an account.

U

Unsecured Loan – A loan not backed by collateral, such as a personal loan or credit card.

W

Wage – An hourly payment made to a worker based on the number of hours worked. Wages differ from salaries, which are fixed regular payments.

Wants – Nonessential items or services that are desirable but not necessary for basic living.

Wealth – The total value of money, property, and other assets owned by a person or household.

Withdrawal – Removing money from a bank account.

Y

Yield – The income earned from an investment, typically expressed as a percentage of the amount invested.

Z

Zero-Based Budgeting – A budgeting method where every dollar of income is assigned a specific purpose—whether it's spending, saving, or investing—so your total income minus total expenses equals zero. It helps you stay in full control of your money by making sure nothing is left unplanned.

Printed in Dunstable, United Kingdom

71169679R00156